Scott Foresman

Assessment Handbook

Grades K-2

Education Resource Center
University of Delaware
Newark, DE 19716-2940

D1516783

PEARSON
Scott Foresman

Editorial Offices: Glenview, Illinois • Parsippany, New Jersey • New York, New York
Sales Offices: Boston, Massachusetts • Duluth, Georgia • Glenview, Illinois
Coppell, Texas • Sacramento, California • Mesa, Arizona

© Pearson Education

ISBN: 0-328-11779-X

Copyright © Pearson Education, Inc.

All Rights Reserved. Printed in the United States of America. The blackline masters in this publication are designed for use with appropriate equipment to reproduce copies for classroom use only. Scott Foresman grants permission to classroom teachers to reproduce from these masters.

12 13 14 15 V001 14 13 12 11 10 09

Contents

© Pearson Education

© Pearson Education

© Pearson Education

Scott Foresman Reading Street Assessment

Some Questions and Answers

This *Assessment Handbook* will be a resource throughout the school year. The handbook presents an overview of our assessment program, and it provides numerous resources in English and in Spanish that you may use to best fit your assessment, instruction, and learning goals. In addition, the *Assessment Handbook* may be regarded as a professional development resource. Inside you will find:

- guidance for using a variety of formal tests and classroom-based assessments;
- proven methods and models for assessing, evaluating, and grading children's work;
- steps for designing quality assessments in all content areas; and
- instructional strategies for preparing children for high-stakes tests.

Scott Foresman Reading Street assessments reflect current theories of teaching language and literacy, and are aligned with solid classroom teaching practices. Formal and informal assessments, combined with "assessable moments" during instruction, become a continuous cycle in which one is always informing and supporting the other, resulting in a seamless learning program for the children.

Following are some commonly asked questions about the *Scott Foresman Reading Street Assessment* Program.

How was the *Scott Foresman Reading Street* formal assessment program developed?

All of the formal assessment components of *Scott Foresman Reading Street* were developed by a specialized testing agency, Beck Evaluation & Testing Associates, Incorporated (BETA). Scott Foresman authorial and editorial staff guided these development activities with respect to specifying the purposes to be served by each component, their general content coverage, and so forth. In addition, Scott Foresman editorial teams critiqued and approved the test specifications and prototype test items for each program element. Finally, Scott Foresman reviewed and provided editorial reactions to all test content. However, the development of all materials was the responsibility of BETA, which also designed and implemented the several field-test or "validation" activities associated with several of the assessment components.

BETA is one of the country's most experienced assessment-development corporations. Over the past twenty years, BETA staff have provided standardized test content for a broad range of state and federal agencies in addition to most leading test and textbook publishers. BETA has played key roles in developing large-scale, high-stakes testing programs in over 20 states. BETA staff regularly assist state departments of education and federal agencies on matters of test development and implementation and on psychometrics, providing such consultation to over

© Pearson Education

33 state Departments of Education. Over the past decade, BETA has developed over 82,000 test items for use in large-scale assessment programs. Most of these programs include the assessment of elementary reading and other language arts. In addition, BETA professionals have facilitated the establishing of student performance standards for 16 state-level assessment programs.

All test items developed by BETA are written by experienced test-development professionals, all with extensive experience at creating test questions in the appropriate content areas and for the targeted grade levels. Most BETA writers have current or prior teaching experience; all writers participating in the *Scott Foresman Reading Street* development activities have several years of experience with test-development activities. BETA editorial staff is made up of highly experienced professionals with advanced degrees and/or certification in reading or language arts. The BETA development activities in support of *Scott Foresman Reading Street* were directed by BETA's senior staff members.

Development activities for this project began with a thorough review of the program scope and components by Michael Beck, BETA's president, and Sheila Potter, BETA's Director of Curriculum Services. This review included a study of program components from the preceding edition of the *Scott Foresman Reading* series as well as plans and prototype materials being evolved for *Scott Foresman Reading Street*. The same two senior staff members participated in discussions with the publisher's senior staff members and their authorial team to review plans for the assessment materials and fine-tune the purposes to be served by the various assessment components. On the basis of this study and series of discussions, BETA outlined the several interrelated assessment publications and began the process of developing test specifications and prototype exercises for each product. Following iterations of review and revision based on comments by senior Scott Foresman editorial personnel, item development began. All test items were written specifically for *Scott Foresman Reading Street;* none were repeated from earlier Scott Foresman reading programs or drawn from generic "item banks." All BETA-developed items were reviewed and edited by two experienced BETA staff members before submission to Scott Foresman editorial review. Based on Scott Foresman's internal editorial review and suggestions, BETA staff then made any required revisions to the materials before they were produced.

There are two critical elements of the assessment-development activities that involved the validation of items. The first had to do with item quality and content alignment. A team of trained raters, trained by personnel from the University of Wisconsin Educational Research Center and directed by Gatti Evaluations, looked at each item on the Unit and End-of-Year Benchmark Tests to verify that the item is of the highest quality and aligns to content with the state curriculum standards of major states.

The second was the empirical field-testing or "validation" of key assessment components in a classroom setting in schools chosen to be representative of the nation's school population. Rather than conducting these tryouts prior to program publication in an unrealistic situation in which the corresponding instructional program was not used, Scott Foresman management made the critical decision to validate the tests as used during the course of their implementation in an actual instructional program. The decision was also made to include excess test material—reading and listening passages and individual test items—in the validation version of these assessments. This

© Pearson Education

permitted BETA psychometric staff and Scott Foresman editorial personnel to select the best-performing subset of items for inclusion in the final versions of the tests. This is a technically superior way of validating tests, rather then revising test items based on field-test data and hoping that the revised versions will be superior to the earlier ones. Such a tryout design also improves the validity of the resulting instruments, as the data collection takes place at the intended point in the school year at which the instruments are to be used. For example, each unit of the Benchmark Tests was piloted immediately following instruction in the assessed content. While this design obviously requires an entire school year for implementation, the resulting assessment components are empirically validated.

How will your program help prepare my students for required state and other standardized tests?

In many ways! The Student Editions, Teacher's Editions, and Practice Books are all carefully crafted to teach the knowledge, skills, and strategies the children need to succeed in all their reading and writing tasks. Many Practice Book pages contain items that reflect common standardized test formats, allowing children repeated opportunities to become familiar with question patterns. In addition, the Weekly Selection Tests and the Unit Benchmark Tests are similarly constructed to provide further practice. Tips on instructional strategies designed to prepare your children for high-stakes tests are described in Chapter 2 of this handbook and in Chapter 4, where they are tailored for English language learners. With the preparation provided by Scott Foresman materials, your students will be ready to face any test-taking situation.

How do I find out where my students are at the beginning of the year?

Finding a starting point for each child can be difficult. Scott Foresman makes it easier by providing test options and parent and learner surveys to help you get to know your students.

Group-administered Baseline Tests give you information about the instructional needs of your class and point you to program features that meet those needs. Diagnostic screening with DIBELS gives you more specific information about children to further refine your instructional plan. Student Surveys familiarize you with each child's reading attitudes and interests, while Parent Surveys give you insights into their literacy habits and behaviors when they are not in school. All of these sources of assessment information work together to help you find a starting point for each child in your class.

How do I know that my students are being tested on the right skills?

Scott Foresman Reading Street is founded on a carefully crafted scope and sequence of skills, based on the most current research and accepted practices in reading instruction, and systematically aligned with national and state language arts and reading standards. Emphasis is placed on the *priority skills,* those skills proven to be indicators of reading success by the National Reading Panel—phonemic awareness, phonics, fluency, vocabulary, and text comprehension.

This scope and sequence is the basis for both the instructional plan and for the depth and breadth of the Scott Foresman Assessment Program. Target skills and strategies are taught in every lesson

© Pearson Education

and then assessed in the Weekly Selection Test. Each target skill is also assessed in the Unit Benchmark Test after it has been taught three times. This systematic coordination of instruction and assessment ensures that children are being tested on *what* they are being taught—in the way they are being taught.

What is the best way to assess my students? How does your program provide what I need?

Accurate and ongoing assessment enables teachers to check children's achievement and growth, to evaluate classroom instruction, and to help children monitor their own learning. An effective assessment system incorporates a variety of assessment methods—both formal and informal—to help teachers meet those varied purposes.

Scott Foresman provides a full complement of materials to meet your assessment requirements. For a formal assessment of unit skills and selections, you'll find several different tests from which to choose. For informal Assessment, the *Assessment Handbook* contains surveys, observation forms, and reporting forms in English and Spanish, as well as questioning and observation techniques you can adapt for your classroom needs. The informal strategies will assist you in making children's self-assessment, peer assessment, portfolios, and grading more efficient. Chapters 2 and 3 of the *Assessment Handbook* describe all of the formal and informal assessments. Also, the Teacher's Edition provides tools for you to make both immediate and long-term decisions about the instructional needs of your students.

How does your program support assessment of my English language learners?

Scott Foresman recognizes the unique challenges and rewards of teaching and assessing the progress of English language learners. Chapter 4 of the *Assessment Handbook* discusses research-based methods of assessing the strengths and needs of English language learners in your classroom. Scott Foresman formal and informal classroom-based assessments reflect those methods as they help teachers monitor growth in the basic reading and expression skills of alphabetic understanding, decoding, sight vocabulary, and grammar, along with measurement of the more complex skills of fluency, comprehension, and vocabulary. The chapter provides guidance on instructional strategies designed to prepare English language learners for formal assessments, including high-stakes tests, as well as advice on appropriate use of accommodations for Scott Foresman formal assessments.

© Pearson Education

Will your program help me when I have to assign grades?

Because we know that grading is a major concern for many teachers, the *Assessment Handbook* contains an entire chapter devoted to grading. You will find guidance on record keeping, designing scoring rubrics, grading children's participation in class discussions and group activities, grading oral presentations, and assessing individual or group writing. The chapter also offers a general discussion of purposes, recommendations, and issues related to grading. Add to this the many formal testing opportunities, which are an integral part of the program, and you have an assessment program that gives you the information you need to meet your assessment requirements.

© Pearson Education

Program Assessment Overview

A variety of assessment instruments, used with fiction and nonfiction selections, allow you to

- determine students' strengths and needs
- monitor students' progress
- measure students' skill and strategy proficiencies
- evalute the effectiveness of instruction

from the beginning of the year to the end!

Baseline Group Tests

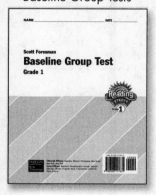

Weekly Selection Tests

Fresh Reads for Differentiated Test Practice

Unit Benchmark Tests

End-of-Year Benchmark Tests

Assessment Handbooks

Technology

© Pearson Education

Beginning of the Year
Diagnose and Differentiate/Establish Baseline Data

Baseline Group Test

- Is administered as a placement test to your entire class
- Provides options for group and individual administration
- Identifies your below-level students requiring strategic intervention
- Identifies your on-level students
- Identifies your above-level students requiring challenge
- Helps you use *Scott Foresman Reading Street* features and components to focus instruction on students' needs
- Establishes baseline data

Assessment Handbook for K–2

Informal classroom-based assessment strategies and tools including:

- Student and Parent Surveys
- Reading, writing, and oral-language Teacher Checklists
- Running Records
- Teacher Observation
- Portfolios

© Pearson Education

During the Year
Monitor Progress/Assess and Regroup

Teacher's Edition

- Ongoing Assessment
- Monitor Progress Boxes
- Student Self-Monitoring
- Guiding Comprehension Questions
- Reading Fluency Assessment
- Reader Response Questions
- Practice for Standardized Tests
- Retelling Scoring Rubrics
- Writing Scoring Rubrics
- Spelling Tests

Practice Book

- Practice pages in standardized test
- Practice skills sure to be on tests
- Helps you identify students needing more instruction

Weekly Selection Tests

- Are administered mid-week
- Contain vocabulary and comprehension sections
- Measure "target" and "review" comprehension skills in the context of authentic literature
- Combine multiple-choice and constructed-response questions about the weekly selections

© Pearson Education

Fresh Reads for Differentiated Test Practice

- Are administered weekly
- Provide a leveled reading selection for below-level, on-level, and advanced-level students
- Give students opportunities to practice the "target" and "review" comprehension skills each week
- Combine multiple-choice and constructed-response questions about the selection

Unit Benchmark Tests

- Are administered at the end of each unit
- Provide one or two new reading selections
- Assess unit "target" and "review" comprehension skills, vocabulary strategies, high-frequency words, phonics skills, and grammar, usage, and mechanics skills, as well as writing
- Combine multiple-choice and constructed-response questions
- Provide an integrated approach to assessment

Assessment Handbook for K–2

Informal classroom-based assessment strategies and tools, including:

- Grading guidance
- On-going teacher observation
- Running records
- Retellings and rubrics
- Teacher-Student Conference Record form
- Reading and Writing Strategy Assessment forms
- Peer Assessment form
- Portfolio logs
- Summary forms

Technology

- Fluency Coach: Oral reading fluency assessment (WCPM) and practice
- Success Tracker: Online assessment and data management with diagnostic prescriptions and alignment to standards
- Exam View: Test generator with alignment to state standards and prescriptions

© Pearson Education

End of the Year
Administer Summative Assessment

End-of-Year Benchmark Test

- Is a cumulative test administered at the end of each grade
- Provides three reading selections
- Tests "target" and "review" comprehension skills, vocabulary strategies, high-frequency words, phonics skills, and grammar, usage, and mechanics skills, as well as writing
- Combines multiple-choice and constructed-response questions
- Provides an integrated approach to assessment

Assessment Handbook for K–2

Informal classroom-based assessment strategies and tools, including:
- Grading guidance
- Teacher-Student Conference Record form
- Reading and Writing Strategy Assessment forms
- Summary forms

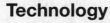

Technology

- Fluency Coach: Oral reading fluency assessment (WCPM) and practice
- Success Tracker: Online assessment and data management with diagnostic prescriptions and alignment to standards
- Exam View: Test generator with alignment to state standards and prescriptions

© Pearson Education

Chapter 1

Assessment Literacy

Classroom teachers make an extraordinary number of decisions every hour of the school day. Four important decisions are:

1. What are the critical understandings and skills that I want the children to know and be able to do upon completion of this lesson/unit/grade?

2. How will I know if the children have accomplished this?

3. What will I do to support those who have not?

4. What will I do to support those who already have?

The critical understandings and skills are the **learning targets**, usually based on school, district, and/or state curriculum standards. The second question is the focus of this introductory section of the handbook. *How will I know? What evidence must I collect?*

While Scott Foresman offers many valuable resources, strategies, and tools for collecting evidence of achievement, educators must be wise about the subject of **assessment** – what it is, when to use it, how to do it, and why it is so important.

What Is Assessment Literacy?

Now, more than ever before, it is important for all teachers and administrators to be "literate" about educational assessment and evaluation. Why? Research tells us that the use of meaningful classroom assessment strategies and tools, such as questioning, observational methods, and student self-assessment, empowers educators, guides instruction, and improves learning.

Further, we cannot ignore that increased demands for accountability at the state and national levels, including Reading First, No Child Left Behind (NCLB), and Adequate Yearly Progress (AYP), have produced an unprecedented proliferation of testing. Children's test performance has become the accountability yardstick by which the effectiveness of schools, districts, states, and even teaching is measured and judged.

To be informed consumers and creators of assessment, individuals must:

• Understand the power of assessment in promoting student achievement

• Become knowledgeable about the functions, strengths, and limitations of formal and informal assessment

• Maintain a balance of summative and formative assessments in their classrooms and schools

• Embrace standards of quality as they evaluate and create assessments

• Use sound assessment practices to design and administer quality classroom-based assessments

© Pearson Education

What Is Assessment?

The Latin root of the word *assess* means "to sit beside." This is a much gentler notion of this concept than most of us have, although "sitting beside" children to confer about the development of a story in progress, to conduct a running record, or to observe a group discussion are valuable assessment techniques.

Assessment is simply the gathering and interpretation of evidence about student learning. There are many methods for collecting information to determine if children have mastered the knowledge and skills, or the learning targets. We can use a variety of formal and informal measures to collect that evidence.

Formal and Informal Measures

Formal assessment measures are most often regarded as tests – tasks presented to children in order to obtain systematic evidence about their performance. The tasks are designed to provide samples of individual achievement and are administered, scored, and interpreted according to prescribed conditions.

Often, formal assessments are regarded as **summative** because they come at the end of an instructional process and are used to determine placement or assign grades. Examples are chapter tests, unit projects, and final examinations. (Airasian 2000)

Standardized tests are formal assessments designed to be administered to large numbers of test takers. Testing conditions, such as precise directions, time allowances, and security procedures, are tightly controlled. The tests are administered at the same time each year. Test questions are written, reviewed, and revised following tryouts by a representative sample of the population for which the instrument is designed.

Examples of standardized tests are commercially published tests, as well as state assessments, which are now used annually to measure student achievement of standards for reporting and accountability purposes, in compliance with federal NCLB legislation and other mandates. These tests are often called "high-stakes," because scores are made very public, and schools and districts are subject to sanctions and embarrassment if they do not make annual AYP goals. (Popham 2004)

Informal Assessment: Dr. Richard Stiggins distinguishes between assessment *of* learning and assessment *for* learning. Assessments *of* learning are generally formal assessments administered at the end of an instructional period. They answer the question "How much have children learned as of a particular point in time?" (Stiggins 2002)

Informal assessment is classroom-based assessment *for* learning that helps us *dig deeper* in order to ascertain exactly *how* individual children are making progress toward achievement of the learning targets.

While these assessment tasks may not be the same type or depth for all children, and may not be recorded in a prescribed, standardized manner, they are not "informal" in the sense of "casual" or "random." Instead, informal assessment is thoughtfully planned and intentional monitoring of learning that takes place *during* the instructional process, rather than the evaluation of learning at the conclusion of the process.

© Pearson Education

Examples of informal assessments are teachers' questions, observations, homework, quizzes, and individual conferences with students. These assessments are often called **formative** assessments because they are influential in "forming" the process under way and are intended to guide and inform instruction.

Balancing Formative and Summative Assessment

Annually administered tests, such as state assessments, provide general feedback about children's performance related to broad content standards, or achievement targets. These tests are not designed to offer the immediate and ongoing information about achievement that teachers need to make critical instructional decisions. Even once-a-unit classroom tests do not provide sufficient information to improve teaching and increase learning. (Stiggins 2004)

> "Balance continuous classroom assessment in support of learning with periodic assessments verifying learning."
> (Stiggins 2002)

To establish and maintain productive, learning-centered classroom environments, teachers rely on a balance of informal assessments *for* learning and formal assessments *of* learning to guide their instruction. They use an array of formative and summative measures *derived from* and/or *aligned with* the curriculum content standards and objectives and based on their assessment purposes.

Why and when do we use formative assessment?

- To diagnose children's strengths and needs

- To elicit prior knowledge for a concept or topic

- To provide frequent feedback to children that is descriptive and helpful, rather than judgmental, as in grades

- To motivate learners to increase effort as they experience incremental successes

- To build children's confidence in themselves as learners

- To help children take responsibility for their learning as they monitor their progress and adjust their goals

- To plan, modify, and regulate the pace of instruction to meet the needs of all children

- To communicate with parents and caregivers (e.g., learning expectations, children's progress in meeting learning targets, and methods of providing support at home)

Why and when do we use summative assessment?

- To report achievement of content standards, or the learning targets

- To document growth over time (e.g., unit-to-unit, year-to-year)

- To assign grades appropriately at the end of a unit or for a report card, for instance

- To validate judgments and decisions about student achievement

© Pearson Education

- To recommend children for promotion and placement in special programs

- To gauge program effectiveness, note strengths, and identify gaps

- To examine comparative data across schools and districts in order to make programmatic decisions (e.g., establish school-improvement priorities, improve curriculum alignment, or establish the need for intervention programs or additional resources)

- To satisfy state and federal accountability mandates, such as AYP

- To inform the public (e.g., tax payers, business leaders, and legislators)

Evaluating Assessments for Quality

Most textbooks and instructional programs, including *Scott Foresman Reading Street,* have accompanying assessments for teachers to use. The formal and informal measures within *Scott Foresman Reading Street* reflect the highest standards of quality and seamlessly align with the instructional program. Teachers may also wish occasionally to construct their own tests and performance assessments for other content areas and interdisciplinary studies.

> "The current model of standards-based reform, so prevalent in the discourse of national and state efforts, positions content standards as the primary driving force behind just about every other educational phenomenon."
>
> (Pearson 2001)

In order to implement fair and sound assessment, teachers are encouraged to consider the following standards for evaluating the quality of commercial assessments and for designing their own classroom assessments to augment or replace the textbook measures.

Know Your Learning Targets

Statewide and district-wide curriculum statements embody the content knowledge and skills we want our children to have, and they are the basis for all our testing. They may be labeled as content standards, benchmarks, learning objectives, expectations, or goals. The main point is *know* what the learning targets are, and teach them to the children.

- "Unpack" the content standards to identify the underlying knowledge, concepts, processes, skills, and dispositions (that is to say, attitudes, values, or habits of mind) that become the **learning targets.**

- Translate the targets into child-friendly language.

- Post the targets in the classroom for all to see.

- Discuss the targets with the children at the beginning of the instructional process (e.g., lesson, unit, or marking period).

- Review them throughout the process so that children have clear, reachable targets to hit.

Determine the Match

Teachers must carefully scrutinize each test item to ensure that the assessment has **content validity.** To what extent does the assessment measure what it is being used

© Pearson Education

to measure? Does the content of the test or task represent a balanced and adequate sampling of the targeted knowledge and skills as they are taught in the classroom? In other words, a recall exercise in which children are to match vocabulary words with their definitions would not be a valid assessment of a vocabulary standard requiring children to use structural analysis and context clues to determine word meanings. Test questions and tasks should clearly reflect the learning targets and require children to perform the behaviors as you have taught them.

Consider the Amount

An effective assessment measures only a modest number of important learning targets and measures them well, so teachers and children are not overwhelmed by the length and complexity of the activity. (Popham 2004) Assessments are meant to sample components of the learning taking place in the classroom, so an appropriate test or task must also contain a sufficient number of items related to each sampled learning target. In this way, teachers can be confident that the results will identify target-skill areas that have been thoroughly taught and those that need improvement.

Strive for Reliability and Fairness

Reliability How trustworthy is this assessment? Can I rely on the scores? Will this assessment give me the same results about the same learning targets every time?

Scoring of selected-response tests is considered quite reliable, and two teachers scoring the same set of multiple-choice tests will probably get the same results, barring a small chance of human error.

Although constructed-response assessments may measure more meaningful learning targets, they are considered less reliable because scoring is based on judgment.

To increase reliability, many states and school districts develop scoring rubrics and train scorers in a thorough, systematic way. Panels of raters score a large number of papers and discuss their scores until they're consistent in their ratings. Some papers are chosen as anchor papers because the raters believe they exemplify score points on the rubric. These papers are then used to guide subsequent scoring sessions, and reliability is improved.

This activity can be replicated at the building level as teachers of the same grade level collaborate to design and score performance assessments, such as end-of-unit projects and presentations.

Fairness Do all children, including those with diverse cultural and linguistic backgrounds, have an equal chance to demonstrate what they know and can do? Have all had the same opportunity to learn the content? Are the directions clear? Is the environment comfortable?

Fairness in assessment is compromised when teachers assess knowledge and skills that have not been taught, or use assessment formats that do not reflect how the learning targets have been taught (e.g., asking for opinions and reasons when the emphasis has been on retelling of facts).

© Pearson Education

Designing Quality Classroom Assessments

Teachers can construct multi-purpose classroom assessments that reflect these standards of quality – validity, reliability, and fairness. Purposes include diagnosing children's strengths and needs; planning, monitoring, and adjusting instruction; and providing feedback to students, parents, and others regarding progress and proficiency. The following design questions are intended to guide educators as they plan and build their own assessments:

1. **What learning target(s) will you assess?**

2. **For which formative or summative purpose(s) is this assessment being administered?**
   - To detect strengths and needs
   - To motivate learners
   - To assign grades
   - To check progress
   - To group for instruction
   - To collect additional evidence
   - To evaluate instruction
   - Other

3. **Who will use the results of this assessment?**
   - Students
   - Teacher(s)
   - Parent(s)
   - Principal
   - Community
   - Other

4. **What format will the assessment take?**

It is important to select the format that most appropriately matches the target. For example, you wouldn't create a multiple-choice test to assess children's use of action verbs in their writing. Rather, you would assign a constructed-response activity asking them to incorporate action verbs in their text.

Conversely, you wouldn't use a constructed-response format to assess children's identification of states and their capitals. An activity requiring them to match states and capitals would suffice for this purpose – assessing recall. Constructed responses are valuable because they help us seek insights into children's reasoning behind their answers or evidence that they can apply what they have learned. Possible assessment formats and examples of activities are listed in the table at the end of this topic.

© Pearson Education

5. What criteria will you use to evaluate performance?

- How will you know it when you see it?

- What does hitting the target look like? What are the qualities?

- Is there one right answer or several possible answers?

- What will you accept as evidence that children have hit the target, that is, that they have acquired the knowledge and skills identified in the content standards?

6. What type of feedback will be provided to guide improvement?

How will results be communicated? How will you tell the story behind the numbers? Will you use a letter grade, a rubric score, written descriptive comments, a checklist, a point on a continuum of learning, such as an oral language behaviors' continuum, or another way?

The most valuable feedback is very specific and descriptive of how the performance hits (or does not hit) the target. Give concrete suggestions rather than vague comments or encouragement, such as "Nice work!" or "You can do better next time!" Share clear examples of successful work with the children, and have them compare their work with the model. Allow children opportunities to revise their performances.

Transforming learning expectations into assessment tasks, assigning criteria, designing scoring procedures, and preparing feedback are challenging and time-consuming activities when they are attempted alone.

It is a rewarding and collegial experience to collaborate with peers in articulating expectations, designing common assessments, analyzing student work, and selecting anchor/model performances. When educators work together to become assessment literate, they empower each other with the ability to improve assessment practices and accountability systems in their school districts and states. More importantly, they increase learning for children.

© Pearson Education

	Assessment Design Options	
Possible Format	**Examples of Tasks**	**Suggested Scoring/Feedback**
Selected Response	• Multiple choice • Matching • True-false	One right answer; cut scores and percentages
Short Constructed Response (written/oral)	• Fill in the blank • Sentence completion • Graphic organizer • Brief response to prompt	One (or few) right answers; cut scores and percentages
Extended Constructed Response (written/oral)	• Prompt-based narrative, descriptive, expository, and persuasive writing • Retellings • Position with support • Summaries	More than one right answer; scoring with checklists, descriptive criteria, standards; continuum, rubrics, comparative models
Performances	• Oral presentation • Demonstration • Discussion • Role play	More than one right answer; scoring with checklists, descriptive criteria, standards, continuum, rubrics, peer and self-evaluation; comparative models
Products	• Science project • Visual display • Model • Video • Poem, story, play • Log/journal • Portfolio	More than one right answer; scoring with checklists, descriptive criteria, standards, continuum, rubrics, comparative models
Processes	• Strategy applications (e.g., think-alouds, questioning) • Teacher-student conferences • Peer and group assessments • Student self-assessments • Interviews • Inventories • Observations • Book club participation • Surveys of reading or writing behaviors • Portfolio entry slips • Response logs • Reading/writing lists	No right answer; do not score; collect as additional evidence; provide descriptive feedback to students

© Pearson Education

What is the *Scott Foresman Reading Street Assessment System?*

All assessments in the program reflect current theories of teaching language and literacy, and are aligned with solid classroom teaching practices. *Scott Foresman Reading Street* offers a seamless assessment cycle at each grade. The formal and informal assessments, combined with assessable moments during instruction, become a continuous cycle where one is always informing the other, resulting in a seamless learning program for the children. Fundamental to the cycle are clear, grade-appropriate, and important learning targets that are aligned with national and state curriculum content standards.

> To prepare students for standardized tests, teachers should teach "the key ideas and processes contained in content standards in rich and engaging ways; by collecting evidence of student understanding of that content through robust local assessments, rather than one-shot standardized testing; and by using engaging and effective instructional strategies that help students explore core concepts through inquiry and problem solving."
>
> (McTighe, Seif, & Wiggins 2004)

- At each grade the cycle begins with the administration of a baseline assessment to establish a starting point for placing children and to determine the amount of instructional support they will need in order to hit the targets. The use of DIBELS (Dynamic Indicators of Basic Early Literacy Skills) allows teachers to diagnose children's specific needs in reading, such as phonemic awareness, alphabetic principle, and fluency.

- Progress is then monitored daily and weekly through informal assessments, such as teacher observations, running records, retellings, and conferencing, as well as formal assessments.

- The Weekly Selection Tests assess children's understanding of the weekly reading selections, and the Fresh Reads for Differentiated Test Practice give children opportunities to practice comprehension and build fluency with new selections matched to their instructional levels.

- The Unit Benchmark Tests and the End-of-Year Benchmark Tests are summative assessments designed to assess children's understanding of the targeted skills, strategies, and critical thinking skills taught throughout the unit and the school year.

What are the assessment targets?

Reading

What are the reading targets? The National Reading Panel was convened to assess the research-based knowledge and effectiveness of various methods of teaching reading. In their 2000 report, the panelists concluded that certain reading skills take priority over others and are essential as children learn to become independent, strategic readers and writers.

Scott Foresman Reading Street emphasizes the **priority skills** that are proven to be indicators of reading success:

© Pearson Education

Phonemic awareness is the ability to identify the separate sounds, or phonemes, that make up spoken words, and to alter and arrange sounds to create new words. It is a subset of phonological awareness, a broad term meaning the awareness of sounds in spoken language. Knowledge of phonemic awareness allows children to hear separate sounds, recognize a sound's position in a word, manipulate sounds, and understand the role sounds play in language. In *Scott Foresman Reading Street,* phonemic awareness instructional and assessment activities include isolating, blending, segmenting, deleting, adding, and substituting phonemes.

Phonics is the study of how letters represent sounds in *written* language, unlike phonemic awareness, which is strictly *oral*. Phonics instruction and assessment in *Scott Foresman Reading Street* include:

- **Print awareness** Understanding the relationship between oral and written language, that written language carries meaning, and that print is read from left to right

- **Alphabetic knowledge** Knowledge of the shapes, names, and sounds of letters

- **Alphabetic principle** Understanding that there is a systematic relationship between sounds (phonemes) and letters (graphemes)

- **Decoding** The process of analyzing letter-sound patterns in words to ascertain meaning

- **Knowledge of high-frequency words** Sometimes called "sight words," these are the words that appear most often in our written language. Because children need to know these words when they read stories and write sentences, these words are introduced before children have learned many letter-sound patterns. Many high-frequency words cannot be decoded easily because of irregular and uncommon letter-sound patterns. Others do conform to phonics rules but must be taught as whole words because children have not yet learned the letter-sound relationships within them.

Fluency is the ability to effortlessly, quickly, and accurately decode letters, words, sentences, and passages. Fluent readers are able to group words into meaningful grammatical units and read with proper expression. Fluency is an essential component of comprehension and is assessed regularly in *Scott Foresman Reading Street.*

> "Priority skills are those instructional goals that are the best predictors of reading success for students at an identified time in their reading growth."
> (Vaughn & Linan-Thompson 2004)

Vocabulary acquisition and development contribute significantly to overall text comprehension. While extensive reading experiences with varied text types and opportunities for classroom discussion are known to increase word knowledge, *Scott Foresman Reading Street* explicitly teaches and assesses vocabulary skills through the study of context clues, word structure, and dictionary/glossary use.

- Context clues from the words or phrases surrounding an unknown word help readers identify its meaning. Context clues include synonyms, antonyms, definitions, explanations, descriptions, and examples that appear within the text surrounding an unfamiliar word.

© Pearson Education

- Study of word structure is the analysis of word-meaning elements to make meaning of the word as a whole. Such meaningful elements include word roots, prefixes, suffixes, and compound words. Syllabication generalizations and inflected endings, which change the tense, case, or singular-plural form of words but do not affect meaning or part of speech, are also taught and assessed.

> "Having a strong vocabulary is not only a school goal, it is a characteristic that allows us to participate actively in our world, and it is viewed by those we meet as the hallmark of an educated person."
> (Blachowicz 2005)

- Understanding what dictionaries/glossaries are and why, when, and how to use them helps to increase children's vocabularies. Children become familiar with the organization and format of dictionaries and glossaries and are guided and assessed in their use of the components of an entry, including syllabication, pronunciation, part of speech, etymology, and definition.

Text comprehension, the overarching goal of reading, is the active process of constructing meaning from text. It is a complex process in which readers apply their prior knowledge and experiences, use their understandings about text (types, structures, features, etc.), and intentionally employ an array of before-, during-, and after-reading strategies and skills in order to attain meaning. Effective readers combine their own experiences with their interpretation of the author's intent as they work to make sense of ideas in text.

In *Scott Foresman Reading Street,* children's use of targeted comprehension strategies and skills is monitored continuously on the Weekly Selection Tests and Fresh Reads for Differentiated Test Practice. Children in first and second grade read a variety of engaging narrative and expository texts and respond to appropriate multiple-choice and constructed-response questions designed to assess how they use the comprehension skills in constructing meaning. (Please note that *listening* comprehension is assessed in kindergarten and is optional in first grade.) There are three types of comprehension questions that correspond to the *In the Book* and *In My Head* categories of questions in the instructional program.

Literal questions focus on ideas explicitly stated in the text, although *not necessarily* verbatim. In response to these items, children *recognize* and *identify* information that might be found in a single sentence or in two or more sentences of contiguous text. Questions for young children in kindergarten through second grade begin as very literal and concrete.

Inferential questions are based on the theme, key concepts, and major ideas of the passage, and often require children to *interpret* information from across parts of the text and to *connect* knowledge from the text with their own general background knowledge. What is considered "inferential" for younger children may actually be "literal" for older children. Throughout the program, children are scaffolded and guided as they move from literal to inferential understanding of text.

© Pearson Education

Critical-analysis questions are also inferential in nature and focus on important ideas in the selection. Yet, they differ from inferential questions in that readers are required to stand apart from the text and *analyze, synthesize,* and/or *evaluate* the quality, effectiveness, relevance, and consistency of the message, rhetorical features (tone, style, voice, etc.), author or character motivation, and the author's purpose or credibility. These questions are introduced in second grade after students demonstrate they can respond to literal and inferential questions.

Writing

Skills include:

- Elaborating on ideas
- Focusing on main idea/topic
- Writing with a personal interest
- Connecting ideas with appropriate order words
- Selecting precise words
- Constructing sentences of various lengths and types
- Controlling mechanical aspects of writing

FORMAL ASSESSMENTS

At grades 1 and 2, **Unit Benchmark Tests** and **End-of-Year Benchmark Tests** require responses to narrative, descriptive, expository, and persuasive writing prompts. The Writing Scoring Rubrics assess six traits:

- Focus/Ideas
- Organization/Paragraphs
- Voice
- Word choice
- Sentences
- Conventions

INFORMAL ASSESSMENTS

- The **Writing Behaviors Checklist** provides information about children's awareness of basic writing concepts and their ability to communicate through writing.

- Written **Retellings** demonstrate children's ability to understand narrative and expository text elements, and to recall and record information in writing.

- **Writing Logs** allow children to monitor their writing growth over time.

- **Writing Strategy Assessments** help teachers synthesize information about children's writing progress and use of writing strategies.

- **Teacher-Student Conferences** provide insights about children's writing behaviors and strategies.

© Pearson Education

- **Student Portfolios,** containing draft and final copies of work, give evidence of children's growth and progress in writing.

Grammar, Usage, and Mechanics

Skills include:

- Sentences
- Parts of speech (i.e., nouns, verbs, adjectives, adverbs, pronouns (contractions), prepositions, conjunctions, and interjections)
- Capitalization, punctuation, and indentation

Skills are assessed through the formal assessments, **Unit Benchmark Tests** and **End-of-Year Benchmark Tests**. The Writing Scoring Rubrics assess sentence structure, fluency, and variety, as well as control of writing conventions.

Speaking and Listening

Skills include:

- Preparing to speak to a group
- Speaking with appropriate purpose
- Speaking with an appropriate delivery and manner
- Listening with appropriate purpose
- Evaluating a speaker's delivery and message

Skills are assessed through the Oral Language Behaviors Checklist. This teacher form allows you to record children's speaking and listening behaviors at the beginning of the year. Other informal assessments that allow you to document children's oral language development throughout the year include oral Retellings, Teacher-Student Conference Records, Ongoing Teacher Observation, and Student Portfolios.

Research/Study Skills

Skills include:

- Understanding and using graphic sources, such as charts, maps, diagrams, graphs, and so on
- Understanding and using reference sources, such as dictionaries, encyclopedias, library databases, and so on
- Understanding and using the research process

Skills are assessed informally by having children demonstrate the ability to perform a task involving the use of the skill.

© Pearson Education

References

Airasian, P. W. *Classroom Assessment: Concepts and Applications.* New York: McGraw-Hill, 2000.

Blachowicz, C. L. Z. "Vocabulary Essentials: From Research to Practice for Improved Instruction." *Research-Based Vocabulary Instruction.* Glenview, IL: Scott Foresman, forthcoming.

McTighe, J.; E. Seif; and G. Wiggins. "You Can Teach for Meaning." *Educational Leadership*, vol. 62, no. 1 (September 2004); pp. 26–30.

National Reading Panel. "Teaching Children to Read: An Evidence-Based Assessment of the Scientific Research Literature on Reading and Its Implications for Reading Instruction." *Reports of the Subgroups.* Bethesda, MD: National Institute for Literacy, National Institute of Child Health and Human Development, 2000.

Pearson, P. D. "Learning to Teach Reading: The Status of the Knowledge Base." In *Learning to Teach Reading: Setting the Research Agenda.* Ed. C.M. Roller, pp. 4–19. Newark, DE: International Reading Association, 2001.

Popham, W. J. "All About Accountability/Tawdry Tests and AYP." *Educational Leadership*, vol. 62, no. 2 (October 2004); pp. 85–86.

Stiggins, R. J. "Assessment Crisis: The Absence of Assessment FOR Learning." *Phi Delta Kappan,* vol. 83, no. 10 (June 2002); pp. 758-765.

———. "New Assessment Beliefs for a New School Mission." *Phi Delta Kappan*, vol. 86, no. 01 (September 2004); pp. 22–27.

Vaughn, S., and S. Linan-Thompson. *Research-Based Methods of Reading Instruction, Grades K–3.* Alexandria, VA: Association for Supervision & Curriculum Development, 2004.

© Pearson Education

Chapter 2 # Formal (Summative) Assessment of Learning

Overview

What is formal, or summative, assessment?

- A systematic method of gathering information about children's knowledge and skills typically based on written tests, each designed for a specific purpose

- Tests designed to provide a sample of individual performance, administered, scored, and interpreted according to prescribed directions

- In *Scott Foresman Reading Street*, a means of determining children's progress at various checkpoints throughout the school year

Why should we use formal assessments?

- Continuous assessment and evaluation are critical to successful teaching and learning.

- Gathering information in a systematic way can be used to validate judgments and decisions about learning.

- Formal assessments provide the same opportunity for each child taking the test.

  - Each child receives the same directions.

  - Each test is scored by the same criteria.

- Feedback from formal assessments enables children to learn about their own literacy development.

- The system of formal assessments supported and enhanced with classroom-based assessments in *Scott Foresman Reading Street* helps teachers to continually refine and modify instruction in the classroom to meet the needs of the children.

> "Tests should be considered nothing more than attempts to systematically gather information. The bottom line in selecting and using any assessment should be whether it helps students."
>
> (Farr 1992)

How does using both formal and informal assessment benefit my students?

- Assessment occurs continuously throughout the day every day in every teacher's classroom. When you ask questions or when you observe children working on an assignment, you are conducting classroom-based assessments.

- The knowledge gained from using both of these forms of assessment together will provide you with a comprehensive picture of your children's skills and abilities.

- Both are quite important, and, when used together, they form a solid basis for making educationally-sound decisions for children.

© Pearson Education

What options are available?

- *Scott Foresman Reading Street* includes a series of formal assessments with differing purposes that provide a range of information about children's proficiency.

What kinds of formal assessments are included in this program?

- Baseline Group Tests (K–1–2)
- DIBELS (K–1–2) (optional)
- Weekly Selection Tests (1–2)
- Fresh Reads for Differentiated Test Practice (1–2)
- Unit Benchmark Tests (K–1–2)
- End-of-Year Benchmark Tests (1–2)

What are the functions of the different kinds of tests?

- Use **Baseline Group Tests** when you need to establish baseline data for determining the level of instructional support children need and placing them into instructional groups.

- Use **DIBELS (Dynamic Indicators of Basic Early Literacy Skills)** to show children's mastery of very specific skills proven to be indicators of reading success.

- Use **Weekly Selection Tests** when you want to assess children's understanding of the content and vocabulary of main selections.

- Use **Fresh Reads for Differentiated Test Practice** to give children an opportunity to practice comprehension skills with a selection matched to each student's instructional level.

- Use **Unit Benchmark Tests** to assess children's understanding of skills, strategies, and critical thinking skills taught throughout the unit.

- Use the **End-of-Year Benchmark Test** to assess children's understanding of skills, strategies, and critical thinking skills taught throughout the year.

Why are there so many different types of tests to administer?

- Reading is complex, involving interactions among reader, text, and context; use of multiple measures provides an accurate and complete picture of the children.

- By having a variety of assessments, you can select the ones that will be most useful for you and the children.

> "No single instrument or technique can adequately measure achievement in reading..."
> (Winograd 1991)

© Pearson Education

Do I have to use all the formal assessments?

Select the tests that meet the assessment needs of your children and align best with your curriculum and instruction.

What instructional strategies will help to prepare the children for formal assessments and high-stakes tests?

- Use the *Scott Foresman Reading Street* program to continually monitor children's progress and refine instruction to reflect their needs.

- Use the administration of the formal assessments as a way to teach test-taking skills.

- Literal, inferential, and critical-analysis questions on the formal assessments are based on the question-answer framework used in instruction and are similar to question types on high-stakes assessments.

- Daily practice in answering, analyzing, and asking Right There, Think and Search, and Author and Me questions will improve children's achievement on high-stakes standardized tests.

- Download and examine released forms of state and standardized assessments, reviewing the various item constructions and test vocabulary. Model and discuss the thinking steps involved in responding to both multiple-choice and constructed-response items.

- Pre-teach the "language of tests" encountered in directions and test items, including:

  - Question words: *who, what, which, where, when, why,* and *how*

  - Emphasis words: *not, except, most likely, probably, main, both, neither, either, most,* and *least*

  - Action words: *tell, answer, mark, describe,* and *support with details*

- Encourage the children to be careful readers and to check their own work.

- Provide repeated opportunities for practicing all the techniques above.

References

Farr, R. "Putting It All Together: Solving the Reading Assessment Puzzle." *The Reading Teacher*, vol. 46, no. 1 (September 1992); pp. 26–37. Reprinted in *Reading Assessment in Practice*. Newark, DE: International Reading Association, 1995.

Winograd, P.; S. Paris; and C. Bridge. "Improving the Assessment of Literacy." *The Reading Teacher*, vol. 45, no. 2 (October 1991); pp. 108–116. Reprinted in *Reading Assessment in Practice*. Newark, DE: International Reading Association, 1995.

© Pearson Education

Baseline Group Test

What is it?	• A placement test given at the beginning of the school year to establish a baseline for each child
Why would I choose it?	• To identify children who are on grade level, those who need intervention, and those who could benefit from more challenge • To recognize how best to shape the curriculum to fit the needs of all children
What does it test?	• In kindergarten, readiness skills (such as understanding left/right directions and location prepositions), letter recognition, phonological awareness (such as initial and final consonant sounds), listening-comprehension skills, and concepts of print are tested. Also included is a graded oral vocabulary test (optional). • In grade 1, phonemic awareness, phonics, letter and word recognition, and listening-comprehension skills are tested. Also included are a graded oral vocabulary test and a passage for testing fluency and/or doing a running record (both optional). • In grade 2, phonemic awareness, phonics, high-frequency words, vocabulary words, and reading-comprehension skills are tested. Also included are a graded oral vocabulary test and a passage for testing fluency and/or doing a running record (both optional).
When do I use it?	• At the beginning of the school year, to establish baselines for children and to place them in groups according to their level of ability • Throughout the year as needed to assess progress and determine instructional requirements of new children
How do I use it?	• Some sections of the test may be group administered. Other sections require an individual administration.
How do I use the results?	• Each test includes a table specifying how many correct responses indicate the various levels of mastery (Strategic Intervention, On-Level, or Advanced Level). • The teacher's manual includes charts with percentage scores, an evaluation chart, and an interpretation key that will allow you to place each child in an appropriate instructional group.

© Pearson Education

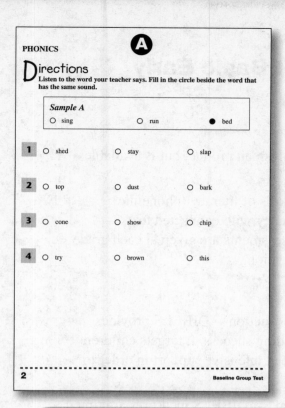

© Pearson Education

PHONICS A

Directions
Listen to the word your teacher says. Fill in the circle beside the word that has the same sound.

Sample A
○ sing   ○ run   ● bed

1 ○ shed   ○ stay   ○ slap

2 ○ top   ○ dust   ○ bark

3 ○ cone   ○ show   ○ chip

4 ○ try   ○ brown   ○ this

2   Baseline Group Test

VOCABULARY B

Directions
Fill in the circle beside the word that best fits in the blank.

Sample E
My cat sleeps _____ my bed.
○ full
● under
○ which

1 The big rock was too _____ to move.
○ loud
○ green
○ heavy

2 My father _____ our house.
○ built
○ thing
○ button

3 Lisa _____ the question.
○ fed
○ pleased
○ answered

4 I will _____ be a baby again.
○ always
○ never
○ without

Baseline Group Test   7

A Phonics items are to be read aloud to children.

B Vocabulary/word recognition items include high-frequency words.

C In grades 1 and 2, children answer comprehension questions about passages that they listen to or read.

Samples are from grade 2 test.

READING COMPREHENSION C

Directions
Read each selection. Then answer the questions that follow. Fill in the circle beside the best answer to each question.

Who Cares?

It was a beautiful summer day in the deep woods. A blue jay named Jay met a robin named Rob. Jay was alone. He wanted someone to play with.

"Do you want to play tag?" he asked Rob.

"No, thank you," said Rob.

Jay frowned. There were no other birds around. "Why not?" he asked.

"Because you are a blue jay and I am a robin," said Rob. He turned away.

Jay thought for a minute. What Rob said was true, but Jay did not give up. "Who cares if we are different?" he asked. "Not me."

Now it was Rob's turn to think. A game of tag did sound like fun.

"Then let's play," said Rob, "and you better fly fast!"

1 You can tell this story is make-believe because
○ it has a happy ending.
○ the birds talk like people.
○ it is about playing a game.

Baseline Group Test   9

---

2 Why does Rob say no to Jay?
○ because the two birds are different
○ because he's afraid of the blue jay
○ because the two birds are alike

3 What is the big idea of the story?
○ Being different doesn't matter.
○ Blue jays are better than robins.
○ Playing tag is not safe.

4 What happens at the end of the story?
○ The robin flies away.
○ The blue jay goes home.
○ The two birds play tag.

10   Baseline Group Test

DIBELS (Dynamic Indicators of Basic Early Literacy Skills)

What is it?

- An optional assessment tool that is not a Scott Foresman product but is available through Scott Foresman

- A set of screening tasks focused on the priority skills of literacy (phonemic awareness, alphabetic principle, accuracy and fluency with connected text, vocabulary, and comprehension). Benchmark assessments are given at each grade level to quickly show which children need intervention.

Why would I choose it?

- To quickly group children who will need extra instruction—DIBELS provides benchmark goals that are highly predictive of reading success. It targets children who need strategic intervention and those who need intensive support in order to be successful.

- To identify those children who "know the material"—DIBELS measures are timed to reflect not only item knowledge, but also fluency and automaticity with those items.

- To show children's mastery of very specific skills proven to be indicators of reading success

- To provide a record of children's continued growth throughout the year

- To provide information that will help you make instructional decisions for individual children and the classroom as a whole

What does the research say?

- Benchmark decisions and at-risk factors were based on information collected from several longitudinal studies including Project CIRCUITS (Center for Improving Reading Competence Using Intensive Treatments Schoolwide), funded by the U.S. Department of Education and the Institute for the Development of Educational Achievement in Eugene, Oregon.

- Reading trajectories are established early. At-risk readers on a low trajectory tend to stay on that trajectory and fall further and further behind. The later children are identified as needing support, the more difficult it is to catch up. (Dynamic Measurement Group, 2004)

- DIBELS results correlate highly with outcome-based assessments. If children score at benchmark levels, they will probably also succeed on state-mandated tests.

- Technical reports, field studies, and a complete bibliography of over sixty studies on DIBELS are available on the DIBELS website: http://dibels.uoregon.edu.

© Pearson Education

What does it test?

- In kindergarten, DIBELS measures phonemic awareness skills (Initial Sound Fluency in the fall and the winter and Phoneme Segmentation Fluency in the winter and the spring), and the alphabetic principle (Nonsense Word Fluency in the winter and the spring).

- In first grade, DIBELS measures phoneme awareness (Phoneme Segmentation Fluency in the fall), the alphabetic principle (Nonsense Word Fluency in the fall, winter, and spring), and vocabulary and comprehension (Oral Reading Fluency and Retell Fluency in the winter and the spring).

- In second grade, DIBELS measures the alphabetic principle (Nonsense Word Fluency in the fall) and vocabulary and comprehension (Oral Reading Fluency and Retell Fluency in the fall, winter and spring).

- DIBELS tasks are timed and all measure fluency. Fluency is important at the letter, sound, word, phrase, and passage level.

- The Word Use Fluency task measures vocabulary and oral language ability at every benchmark in every grade; this task is optional.

How do I use it?

- Individually administer grade-appropriate benchmark tasks three times per year to monitor children and catch those at risk of failure.

- Use alternate progress-monitoring forms more frequently to monitor the success of interventions with at-risk children.

- Allow 10–15 minutes per child to administer benchmark tasks three times per year.

- Use the DIBELS website to generate student and class reports.

When do I use it?

- Administer benchmark tasks to all children in the fall, winter and spring, typically September, January and May.

- Use progress-monitoring alternate forms of DIBELS tasks to assess at-risk children more frequently (monthly, bi-monthly, or weekly) to see if specific instructional interventions are working.

How do I use the results?

- Look at entire class results to determine specific areas where most children are weak, and adjust teaching for those weak areas systematically and explicitly.

- Use results to aid in the formation of flexible groups.

- Use results to focus and plan instruction for flexible groups and for individuals.

- Use progress-monitoring results to adjust and refocus instruction on a regular basis.

- Use results to celebrate and inform children and parents about progress.

© Pearson Education

Weekly Selection Tests

What are they?
- Tests taken by children in grades 1 and 2 designed to measure children's understanding of the content and vocabulary of the reading selections in *Scott Foresman Reading Street*
- Tests consisting of multiple-choice and constructed-response questions

Why would I choose them?
- To assess children's understanding of what they read on a frequent basis
- To assess children's understanding of the vocabulary words and target comprehension skill of the week
- To monitor children's progress during the week so that instruction can be modified if necessary

What do they test?
- Understanding of vocabulary words taught in a reading selection
- Comprehension of the reading selection through literal, inferential, and critical-analysis questions (NOTE: Critical-analysis test items are used only at grade 2.)
- Use of reading skills and strategies taught in conjunction with the reading selection

When do I use them?
- Throughout the school year, typically mid-week after children have read a selection

How do I use them?
- The tests are designed to be group administered.

How do I use the results?
- To identify children who can successfully construct meaning from a reading selection and to identify which children need intervention
- To identify the specific comprehension skills a child has and has not mastered

© Pearson Education

Name _____

HIGH-FREQUENCY WORDS

Directions
Read each sentence. Mark the ○ for the word that fits.

1 Let's go to the park _____.

○ very ○ today ○ tall

2 I will do _____ I can to help.

○ whatever ○ begin ○ close

3 She _____ a fish at the lake.

○ lived ○ drove ○ caught

4 I don't _____ that story!

○ when ○ draw ○ believe

5 Pablo has _____ playing all day.

○ been ○ could ○ walked

6 Dinner is _____ done!

○ warm ○ finally ○ hear

© Pearson Education 2

Selection Test   Unit 3 Week 3

7 It is going to snow _____.

○ gone ○ our ○ tomorrow

COMPREHENSION

Directions
Read each question. Mark the ○ for the answer.

8 Where did Anansi meet Turtle?
○ by the river
○ at the Justice tree
○ in Turtle's house

9 Which happened last?
○ Turtle caught a fish.
○ Anansi went to see Warthog.
○ Anansi caught a fish.

10 How did Anansi realize Turtle had cheated him?
○ Anansi was very tired.
○ Anansi did not get full.
○ Warthog told Anansi.

© Pearson Education 2

GO ON

50

Selection Test   Unit 3 Week 3

A Children are tested on all vocabulary words in a selection.

B Comprehension items cover selection content as well as target skill.

© Pearson Education

Samples are from grade 2 Unit 3 test.

Fresh Reads for Differentiated Test Practice

What are they?
- Tests that give children in grades 1 and 2 an opportunity to practice the comprehension skills of the week with a new selection, a "fresh read," matched to each child's instructional reading level
- Tests consisting of multiple-choice and constructed-response questions

Why would I choose them?
- To assess children's abilities to derive meaning from new selections that are at their instructional reading levels
- To retest a child's reading after administering the Weekly Selection Tests
- To check a child's reading rate

What do they test?
- The target and review comprehension skills and strategies for the week
- Comprehension of the reading selection through literal, inferential, and critical-analysis questions (NOTE: Critical-analysis test items are used only at grade 2.)

When do I use them?
- Throughout the year, usually once a week after children have read a new selection aligned to their instructional level

How do I use them?
- The written tests are designed to be group administered.
- Teachers choose which of the three leveled reading passages for the week to give to each child (Strategic-Intervention, On-Level, or Advanced).
- Fluency checks are administered individually.

How do I use the results?
- To gather additional information about a child's ability to comprehend a passage written at his/her instructional reading level
- To gather additional information about the specific comprehension skills a child has and has not mastered
- To monitor a child's progress in fluent reading

© Pearson Education

Name _____

Read the selection. Then answer the questions that follow.

How to Grow a Plant

Orhan got a new plant. He put the plant in his room. The plant did not grow.

He asked his mother, "Why is my plant not growing?"

His mother told him why. A new plant needs water. Water helps it grow. A new plant needs sun. The sun helps it grow.

Orhan put his plant outside in the sun. He gave it water every day. Now Orhan's plant is growing. His plant is big and tall.

Turn the page.

Fresh Reads   Unit 3 Week 3 SI   73

Name _____

Read the selection. Then answer the questions that follow.

The Hill

This year Dennis got a skateboard for his birthday. He jumped for joy because it was something that he had wanted for a long time. He put on his helmet and knee pads and then ran outside to play with it. He lived on a street that had no hills, so he had to push off the ground with one foot to make the board roll forward. Dennis loved playing with his skateboard.

This was fine for a while, but Dennis soon got bored. So Dennis decided to take his skateboard to his friend Jerry's house. Jerry lived on a street that had a big hill. However, when Dennis got ready to go down the hill, he suddenly felt afraid. He knew that going down the high hill could be dangerous. So Dennis went back to his own street. He was happy that he lived on a street with no hills.

Turn the page.

Fresh Reads   Unit 3 Week 3 A   77

(A)

Name _____

Read the selection. Then answer the questions that follow.

(C)

Cheer Up!

Hilde was sick with a bad cold. She was in a bad mood because she	15
hated to be sick. When Hilde's mother asked if she wanted some soup,	28
Hilde answered, "No!" Hilde was not very nice when she was sick.	40
Then her friend Arnold visited. Arnold had a cold too, but he was	53
happy. He did not feel mad when he was sick.	63
When Hilde's mother asked Arnold if he wanted soup, he answered,	74
"Yes, please!" Arnold was nice even though he was sick.	84
Hilde asked Arnold, "How can you be happy when you are sick?"	96
Arnold answered, "You can be happy any time if you try, because	108
life is better when you are happy."	115
After that, Hilde tried to be happy even when she was sick. She also	129
tried to be nice even when she was not sick. She learned that Arnold	143
was right. She learned that everything was better when she tried to be	156
happy.	157

Fresh Reads   Unit 3 Week 3 OL

(B)

Answer the questions below.

1 Why was Hilde unhappy at the beginning of the story?
○ She was sick with a cold.
○ She did not like to do homework.
○ Arnold came to see her.

2 Why was Arnold nice to Hilde's mother?
○ He was very hungry.
○ He felt sorry for her.
○ He was always nice.

3 You can tell that it is often easier for people to be nice when they are
○ happy.
○ sick.
○ sad.

4 Hilde decided to be nice even when she was sick because
○ she wanted to eat soup.
○ she saw that Arnold could do it.
○ she wanted to please her mother.

5 Why was life better for Hilde when she tried to be nice?
_____
_____
_____
_____
_____

76   Fresh Reads   Unit 3 Week 3 OL

A Selections of different ability levels

B Questions on the target skill and review skill of the week

C Opportunity for fluency check

Samples are from grade 2 Unit 3 test.

© Pearson Education

Unit Benchmark Tests

What are they?
- Tests designed to measure the children's ability to apply the target comprehension skills and other skills taught during the unit to a new reading selection

Why would I choose them?
- To assess children's understanding and use of specific skills
- To identify skill areas in which children need intervention and continued practice
- To know that there are sufficient items per individual skill to track a child's proficiency with that skill

What do they test?
- **In kindergarten,** letter naming, phonological awareness, phonemic awareness, phonics, high-frequency word knowledge, listening comprehension, word reading, and writing
- **In grade 1**, unit comprehension skills through literal and inferential questions, high-frequency words, phonics, grammar, usage, and mechanics skills, ability to respond to a writing prompt, and reading fluency (optional)
- **In grade 2,** unit comprehension skills through literal, inferential, and critical-analysis questions, high-frequency words, phonics, vocabulary strategies and skills, grammar, usage, and mechanics skills, ability to respond to a writing prompt, and reading fluency (optional)

When do I use them?
- Throughout the year, at the end of each unit

How do I use them?
- The kindergarten tests can be individually or group administered, while the grade 1 and grade 2 tests are designed to be group administered.
- The optional fluency checks in grade 1 and 2 are individually administered.

How do I use the results?
- For kindergarten, to determine what level of instruction to provide
- To identify children who can successfully construct meaning from a reading selection and to identify children who need intervention

© Pearson Education

PART 1: COMPREHENSION

A

Directions
Many things start to happen in spring. Read about them. Then answer Numbers 1 through 7.

Is It Spring?

Squirrel looked out from the tree.
"Is it spring?" he asked.
"It isn't cold any more," said Bird.

2

Benchmark Test Unit 3

Samples are from grade 1 Unit 3 test.

B

1 What did Bird do at the end of the story?
○ She flew to see Squirrel.
○ She looked for a place for a nest.
○ She crawled around the tree.

2 How are Squirrel, Bird, and Caterpillar the same?
○ They are all happy it is spring.
○ They all want to see their friends.
○ They all need to eat leaves.

3 How are Bird and Caterpillar different?
○ Bird needs to eat leaves.
○ Bird likes the spring.
○ Bird needs to make a nest.

4 What did Squirrel do first?
○ He ate leaves from the tree.
○ He looked out from the tree.
○ He ran to the ground.

5 How did the animals know it was spring?
○ The grass was green.
○ It was raining.
○ They saw flo

6

PART 4: GRAMMAR, USAGE, MECHANICS

C

Directions
Fill in the circle for your answers for Numbers 35 through 40.

35 Which word is a verb?
○ eat
○ always
○ old

36 He _____ the horse.
○ rided
○ ride
○ rides

37 They _____ to go to the p
○ wants
○ wanting
○ want

38 Which one tells what is happening
○ She looks out the window.
○ She looked out the window.
○ She was looking out the window.

PART 5: WRITING

D

PROMPT

In "Is It Spring?" the animals see flowers growing. Think of what it's like outside in the spring. Write to tell what spring is like.

CHECKLIST FOR WRITERS

_____ Did I think about spring before I started to write?

_____ Did I tell what spring is like?

_____ Did I use sense words to tell about things I can see, hear, smell, taste, or touch in the spring?

_____ Do my sentences make sense?

_____ Do my sentences begin with capital letters?

_____ Do my sentences end with end marks?

_____ Did I check my spelling?

_____ Did I make sure my paper is the way I want readers to read it?

Benchmark Test Unit 3   23

A Children read selections in a variety of genres.

B Children respond to multiple-choice and writing questions.

C High-frequency words, phonics, vocabulary skills, and grammar, usage, and mechanics skills are tested.

D Children produce original compositions relating selections in test to unit themes and writing instruction.

© Pearson Education

End-of-Year Benchmark Test

What is it?

- A test designed to measure first and second graders' proficiency at specific skills taught throughout the school year
- A test consisting of multiple-choice and constructed-response questions

Why would I choose it?

- To assess children's understanding and use of specific skills
- To identify skill areas in which children need intervention and continued practice
- To measure children's understanding through an approach that integrates reading, writing, and themes in literature

What does it test?

- Comprehension skills through literal, inferential, and critical-analysis questions
- Phonics
- High-frequency words in grade 1 and vocabulary strategies and skills in grade 2
- Grammar, usage, and mechanics skills
- Ability to respond to a writing prompt
- Ability to make cross-text connections
- Application of learning to a new situation

When do I use it?

- When children have completed all units in their textbook, usually at the end of the school year

How do I use it?

- The test is designed to be group administered.

How do I use the results?

- To diagnose and record individual children's needs for the following school year
- To inform and improve the delivery of curriculum and instruction
- To determine children's overall grades
- To provide helpful feedback to children and parents
- To guide parents in working with their children during vacation, so learning continues throughout the summer months

© Pearson Education

PART 1: COMPREHENSION

A

Directions
Paco's favorite toy is missing! Read about how Paco's sister and mother look for the toy. Then answer Numbers 1 through 7.

Where Is Bear?

Rosa's baby brother, Paco, had a favorite toy bear. He took it every place he went.

One day Rosa's mother said, "I can't find Bear. I thought Bear was in Paco's bag. Now Bear isn't there. Paco will be very sad."

Rosa's mother said, "Rosa, I need your help to look for Bear. Let's think like detectives. Where are the places that Paco goes with Bear?"

2   Benchmark Test   End-of-Year

B

1   **Where were Rosa and her mother?**
- ○ in Paco's school
- ○ at their house
- ○ at the toy store

2   **At the end of the story, why did Rosa and her mother laugh?**
- ○ Paco had Bear the whole time.
- ○ Bear was in Paco's bag after all.
- ○ Paco told them a funny story.

3   **"Where Is Bear?" would be a make-believe story if**
- ○ Bear had been in the toy box.
- ○ Rosa had a baby sister.
- ○ Bear could run and play.

4   **Which of these is best as another good name for this story?**
- ○ "Paco Is Sad"
- ○ "Rosa Finds Bear"
- ○ "Mother and Her Bear"

5   **What did Rosa learn in this story?**
- ○ Some things cannot be found.
- ○ It can help to work together.
- ○ Mothers know everything.

6   Benchmark Test   End-of-Year

Samples are from grade 1 end-of-year test.

PART 4: GRAMMAR, USAGE, MECHANICS

C

Directions
Fill in the circle for your answer choice for Numbers 52 through 60.

52   Which sentence is written correctly?
- ○ Dinner Max wants.
- ○ Max wants to eat dinner.
- ○ Max dinner wants to.

53   We went to see a play on saturday.
Choose the word that should begin with a capital letter.

     see   play   saturday
     ○   ○   ○

Mark the word that best fits in each sentence.

54   We _____ going to the park now.
     are   were
     ○   ○

55   They have the _____ house in th
     smallest   smaller
     ○   ○

28

A   Children read selections in a variety of genres.

B   Children respond to multiple-choice and writing questions.

C   High-frequency words, phonics, vocabulary skills, and grammar, usage, and mechanics skills are tested.

D   Children produce original compositions relating selections in test to unit themes and writing instruction.

D

PART 5: WRITING

PROMPT

In "The Hale Boys Build a Car" and "Riding a Horse," the children become old enough to do something new. Think about something new that you have learned to do this year. Write a story about a new thing you did this year. Tell how it made you feel.

CHECKLIST FOR WRITERS

_____ Did I plan my story before I started writing?

_____ Does my story tell about something new I learned this year?

_____ Does my story tell how doing something new made me feel?

_____ Does my story have a beginning, middle, and end?

_____ Does my story make sense?

_____ Do my sentences begin with capital letters?

_____ Do my sentences end with end marks?

_____ Did I check my spelling?

_____ Did I make sure my paper is the way I want readers to read it?

30   Benchmark Test   End-of-Year

© Pearson Education

© Pearson Education

Chapter 3

Classroom-based Informal Assessment Strategies and Tools

Overview

What is classroom-based assessment?

- A way to determine children's progress based on a regular process of observing, monitoring, and judging the quality of their work

- A system for examining children's work that focuses on formative and summative measures other than formal tests

- A strong basis for instructional decision making

- A means of helping children learn how to make judgments about the quality of their own work

What are the purposes of classroom-based assessments?

- To identify mastery

- To engage children and help develop positive attitudes

- To stress application and other reasoning skills

- To communicate progress to parents

- To identify areas in need of improvement

- To encourage children's self-assessment and evaluation

- To adjust instructional approaches (McMillan 2001)

Why is classroom-based assessment so important?

- A formal assessment administered at the end of an instructional unit works like a snapshot of a moving body—capturing a moment in time. Because children's performance levels change rapidly at times, multiple assessments, similar to an album of snapshots or a video, are necessary.

- High-quality work is most reliably achieved in small, consistent increases that occur over time. The goal is continuous improvement.

> "…quality is the result of regular inspections (assessments) along the way, followed by needed adjustments based on the information gleaned from the inspections."
> (McTighe 1997)

- Teachers can guide children's learning better if they have up-to-date understanding of the children's current performance levels—wasting no time on skills children have already attained and focusing instead on the weaker areas.

- Frequent assessments give *all* children a more equitable opportunity to demonstrate their skills.

What techniques and tools are available?

Questioning Strategies (See pages 51–52)

- The ability to frame and ask powerful questions is an effective instructional and assessment strategy.

- Skillful questioning helps children recall what they know about a topic.

- Questions that require children to analyze information promote in-depth learning.

> "Any decision of consequence deserves more than one piece of evidence."
>
> (Pearson 1998)

Tools for Getting to Know Your Students (See pages 53–60)

- Recording observations on forms and checklists and administering surveys at the beginning of the school year helps you:
    - identify children's interests and attitudes about literacy
    - assess instructional and motivational needs of individual children
    - assess instructional needs of the class as a whole
    - learn specifics about children with particular needs, such as English language learners
    - make good instructional decisions

Ongoing Teacher Observation (See pages 61–69)

- Promotes continuous monitoring of children's performance in the context of classroom activities

- Is grounded in the belief that children seldom attain their highest level of achievement in their first attempt

- Provides children with helpful feedback because it addresses learning while in progress, rather than after the fact

Student Portfolios (See pages 70–76)

- Portfolios provide a place to organize and keep the evidence of the children's progress.

- Portfolios involve children in self-assessment; they evaluate portions of their own work and set goals for improvement.

- Portfolios usually contain children's annotations, or "entry slips," identifying what each entry demonstrates—the basis for its inclusion in the portfolio.

- Portfolios of children's work are better when they result from a combination of "teacher direction and student selection." (Bailey and Guskey 2001)

- Portfolios may be organized in a number of different ways:

© Pearson Education

- A gathering of products from a set of performance tasks

- A collection of representative stages of work for certain products

- A chronological representation of a learner's skill development in a subject or specific area of performance

- Ascending order of quality to show growth over time (Danielson and Abrutyn 1997)

- Descending order of quality to showcase highest quality work first time (Danielson and Abrutyn 1997)

- A self-selected organization based on the child's intended use for the portfolio—perhaps to highlight specific skills

Teacher Summary Reports (See pages 77–82)

- Use observation sheets and other record forms to document and keep cumulative accounts of children as learners.

What are some typical classroom-based assessment activities?

- Class discussions

- Speeches, oral readings, dramatizations, retellings

- Drawings, sculpture, and other artwork

- Graphic organizers

- Collaborative activities and projects

- Student writing, such as stories, reports, and response logs

Where do I find classroom-based assessment activities in *Scott Foresman Reading Street?*

"...mechanisms [of accountability] that provide a variety of means for communicating with parents, administrators, and other members of the community about students' learning . . . such as teacher interpretations of students' learning based on individual work samples . . . seem much more likely to produce the kind of culture of teaching and learning that appears to be critical to improvements in student achievement than are the various external accountability mechanisms that currently predominate."

(Wixson 2004)

- The following teacher's edition features provide a variety of good opportunities to informally assess children:

- Monitor Progress Boxes

- Strategy Self-Check

- Guiding Comprehension Questions

- Monitor Reading Fluency

- Reader Response Questions

- Practice for Standardized Tests

- Retelling Scoring Rubrics

- Writing Scoring Rubrics

- Spelling Tests

© Pearson Education

When do I use these assessment activities?

- Use activities throughout the school year that measure children's growth and development to:
  - make instructional decisions about what to do next
  - help children check their progress
  - determine short-term instructional groupings (guided reading groups, for example)
  - help in differentiating instruction
  - check the effectiveness of instructional strategies

References

Afflerbach, P. *Reading Assessment and Accountability: Helping Children Learn to Self-assess Their Reading.* Presented at the CIERA Summer Institute, 2001.

Bailey, J. M., and T. R. Guskey. "Implementing Student-Led Conferences." In *Experts in Assessment Series.* Ed. T. R. Guskey, and R. J. Marzano. Thousand Oaks, CA: Corwin Press, Inc., 2001.

Danielson, C., and L. Abrutyn. *An Introduction to Using Portfolios in the Classroom.* Alexandria, VA: ASCD, 1997.

Gambrell, L. B., P. S. Koskinen, and B. A. Kapinus. "Retelling and the Reading Comprehension of Proficient and Less-Proficient Readers." *Journal of Educational Research*, vol. 84 (1991), pp. 356–363.

Gambrell, L. B., W. Pfeiffer, and R. Wilson. "The Effects of Retelling Upon Reading Comprehension and Recall of Text Information." *Journal of Educational Research*, vol. 78 (1985), pp. 216–220.

Keene, E. O., and S. Zimmermann. *Mosaic of Thought.* Portsmouth, NH: Heinemann, 1997.

McMillan, J. H. "Essential Assessment Concepts for Teachers and Administrators." In *Experts in Assessment Series.* Ed. T. R. Guskey, and R. J. Marzano. Thousand Oaks, CA: Corwin Press Inc., 2001.

McTighe, J. "What Happens Between Assessments?" *Educational Leadership*, vol. 54, no. 4 (1997); pp. 6–12.

Morrow, L. M. "Effects of Structural Guidance in Story Retelling on Children's Dictation of Original Stories." *Journal of Reading Behavior*, vol. 18, no. 2 (1986); pp. 135–152.

Moss, B. "Teaching Expository Text Structures Through Information Trade Book Retellings." *The Reading Teacher*, vol. 57, no. 8 (May 2004); pp. 710–718.

Pappas, C. C. "Fostering Full Access to Literacy by Including Information Books." *Language Arts*, vol. 68, no. 6 (October 1991); pp. 449–462.

Pearson, P. D. "Instruction and Assessment: Synergistic Energies or a Dysfunctional Family?" Presented at University of California, Berkeley, March 23, 1998.

Raphael, T. E. "Teaching Question Answer Relationships, Revisited." *The Reading Teacher*, vol. 39, no. 6 (February 1986); pp. 516–522.

Wixson, K. K., and M. N. Yochum. "Research on Literacy Policy and Professional Development: National, State, District, and Teacher Contexts." *Elementary School Journal*, vol. 105, no. 2 (November 2004); pp. 219–242.

© Pearson Education

Grades K–2 Classroom-based Assessment: Techniques and Tools

Questioning Strategies

Why is questioning important?

- While asking questions is a routine practice for teachers, it is often overlooked as our most powerful tool for instruction and assessment.

- Artfully crafted questions engage children, focus their attention, stimulate their thinking, facilitate their understanding, and deepen their comprehension.

- Student self-generated questions improve learning and strengthen problem-solving and critical-thinking skills.

How do I use effective questioning strategies?

- Selectively choose questions for specific purposes (e.g., recall-level questions about sequence of ideas and analytic questions about the theme of a story).

- Ask questions that represent diverse thinking activities—recall, analysis, comparison, inference, and evaluation.

- Design questions that emphasize both content and the thinking needed to process the content, using such verbs as *list, define, compare, conclude,* and *defend.*

> "Our questions help us formulate our beliefs about teaching and learning, and those beliefs underlie our instructional decisions."
> (Keene & Zimmermann 1997)

- Remember that when children are asked to analyze information, they will learn more than if asked simply to recall or identify information.

- Listen carefully to children's answers in order to shape skillful follow-up questions.

- Ask probing follow-up questions that help children extend their thinking and clarify and support their points of view.

- Allow wait time because it gives children time to think and provides answering opportunities for those who process more slowly.

- Model question-asking and question-answering behavior, and provide repeated opportunities for children to practice generating their own questions.

- Model questioning with a variety of texts, and, through reading conferences with the children, monitor their developing use of questioning.

- Guide children in understanding that through their own questions, they can actively regulate their reading and learning.

© Pearson Education

How does *Scott Foresman Reading Street* support effective questioning practices?

- Questioning strategies are based on a question-answer framework suggesting an interaction among the question, the text to which it refers, and the prior knowledge of the reader. (Raphael, 1986)

- Children are taught that answering comprehension questions in class and on tests demands thinking; they have to analyze the questions in order to provide the right answers.

- Children learn that answers to questions can be found **In the Book** and **In My Head.**

- **In the Book** questions can be:

  - **Right There** questions, which are *literal* and focus on ideas explicitly stated in the text. The words in the question may match the words in the passage.

  - **Think and Search** questions, which are also *literal* and require children to locate and integrate information from within different sections of the text.

- **In My Head** questions can be:

  - **Author and Me** questions, which are *inferential* in nature, requiring children to interpret information and connect themes and major ideas with their own background knowledge. The most demanding Author and Me questions necessitate use of *critical analysis* as readers evaluate and justify the purpose, content, and quality of text.

  - **On My Own** questions are not based on the text and can be answered from the children's general background knowledge and experience. These questions are often posed by teachers in order to activate prior knowledge before reading and/or to extend the learning beyond the lesson.

- The *Scott Foresman Reading Street* formal assessments offer children a variety of engaging narrative and expository texts, and children respond to test items designed to assess how they use their comprehension skills in constructing meaning.

- Literal, inferential, and critical-analysis questions on the formal assessments are based on the question-answer framework used in instruction and are similar to question types on high-stakes assessments.

- Daily practice in answering, analyzing, and asking Right There, Think and Search, and Author and Me questions will improve children's achievement on high-stakes standardized tests.

© Pearson Education

Getting to Know Your Students

What is the purpose?

- To help you get to know your students and find a starting point in order to make good instructional decisions

- To help you gather information about children's reading, writing, and oral language behaviors at the beginning of the year

- To gather specific information about children with particular needs, such as English language learners

What are my choices?

- Learn about children's interests

  - Have children complete a survey about their interests.

  - Have parents or caregivers complete a survey about their child's interests.

- Learn about children's needs using checklists to

  - Understand children's book and print awareness

  - Evaluate children's facility with reading and writing

  - Note children's oral language behaviors

  - Determine the level of children's English proficiency

- Record what you have learned

  - Record the information you've gathered on the Student Portfolio Sheet.

When do I gather the information?

- During the first few weeks of the school year

How do I use the information?

- Use any or all the provided materials to help you do the following:

  - Assess instructional and motivational needs of individual children

  - Customize your instruction to meet the interests and needs of all the children in your classroom

  - Group children according to their different starting points

© Pearson Education

Teacher Form
Knowledge About Books and Print

What is it?	• A brief survey of a child's familiarity with books and print
What does it show?	• A child's understanding of what a book is and how to handle it • A child's awareness of print
How do I use it?	• Start using this form at the beginning of the year, as you begin shared reading with kindergartners and first graders. • Begin with those children who are not joining in or who seem confused. Work with them individually. • "Share" a book in an encouraging way and let the child handle the book as naturally as he or she can. • Repeat this assessment periodically (every month or so) to monitor the child's progress. Record your observations. • Attach the completed form to the Student Portfolio Sheet. • Consider using the form during parent conferences.

A Checklist format is easy to interpret.

B Space is provided to include other behaviors you may want to track.

Teacher Form
Knowledge About Books and Print

Child Lee Thompson   Date 9/19

Behavior	Yes	Not Yet	Comments
Knows how to hold book right side up	✓		
Knows how to turn pages sequentially, front to back	✓		
Knows that books have titles, authors, and illustrators		✓	
Makes predictions from title, cover, and illustrations		✓	
Can differentiate between pictures and text	✓		starts at left, but at bottom of page
Knows that text and pictures relate to each other	✓		
Tracks print from left to right and top to bottom		✓	
Knows that print represents spoken words	✓		
Knows that there are spaces between words	✓		
Joins in reading text with a familiar, repetitive, or predictable pattern		✓	
After multiple class readings, revisits the book, "reading" the story independently	✓		went back to look at a favorite class book
Other:			

Form for reproduction is on page 102.
Spanish form for reproduction is on page 128.

© Pearson Education

Reading Behaviors Checklist

What is it?	• A form to record your observations of children's reading behaviors at the beginning and throughout the year
What does it show?	• Children's awareness of print and word concepts
	• Children's knowledge of phonological awareness and phonics
How do I use it?	• Complete this form as you observe children dealing with print materials.
	• Use your observations to assess children's needs and to make instructional decisions.
	• Attach the completed form to the Student Portfolio Sheet as additional information about the child.

A Checklist format is quick to complete and easy to interpret.

B Checklist includes all important aspects of a child's early reading behaviors.

C "Not Applicable" column makes checklist adaptable to different grade levels.

Form for reproduction is on page 103.
Spanish form for reproduction is on page 129.

© Pearson Education

3 • Informal Assessment

Teacher Form
Reading Behaviors Checklist

Child **Kristen Cleaver** **A** Date **9/16**

Behavior	Yes	No	Not Applicable
Recognizes letters of the alphabet **B**	✓		**C**
Recognizes name in print	✓		
Recognizes some environmental print, such as signs and logos	✓		
Knows the difference between letters and words	✓		
Knows the difference between capital and lowercase letters	✓		
Understands function of capitalization and punctuation	✓		
Recognizes that book parts such as cover, title page, and table of contents offer information		✓	
Recognizes that words are represented in writing by specific sequences of letters	✓		
Recognizes words that rhyme	✓		
Distinguishes rhyming and nonrhyming words	✓		
Knows letter-sound correspondences	✓		
Identifies and isolates initial sounds in words	✓		
Identifies and isolates final sounds in words	✓		
Blends sounds to make spoken words	✓		
Segments one-syllable/two-syllable spoken words into individual phonemes	✓		
Reads consonant blends and digraphs			✓
Reads and understands endings such as -es, -ed, -ing			✓
Reads vowels and vowel diphthongs			✓
Reads and understands possessives			✓
Reads and understands compound words			✓
Reads simple sentences	✓		
Reads simple stories		✓	
Understands simple story structure	✓		
Other:			

Writing Behaviors Checklist ✓

What is it?
- A form to record your observations of children's writing behaviors at the beginning of the year

What does it show?
- Children's awareness of basic writing concepts
- Children's ability to communicate through writing

How do I use it?
- Complete this form as you observe children drawing and/or writing.
- Use your observations to assess children's needs and to make instructional decisions.
- Attach the completed form to the Student Portfolio Sheet as additional information about the child.

A Checklist format is quick to complete and easy to interpret.

B Checklist includes all important aspects of a child's early writing behaviors.

C "Not Applicable" column makes checklist adaptable to different grade levels.

Form for reproduction is on page 104.
Spanish form for reproduction is on page 130.

Teacher Form
Writing Behaviors Checklist ✓

Child: Kristen Cleaver   **A**   Date 9/28

Behavior	Yes	No	Not Applicable
Produces detailed and relevant drawings	✓		
Dictates messages for others to write **B**	✓		**C**
Writes using scribble, drawing, or letterlike forms	✓		
Distinguishes between writing and drawing	✓		
Writes own name and other important words	✓		
Writes all letters of the alphabet, capital and lowercase		✓	
Writes labels or captions for illustrations and possessions	✓		
Writes messages that move from left to right and top to bottom		✓	
Uses phonological knowledge to map sounds to letters when writing		✓	
Holds pencil and positions paper correctly	✓		
Uses basic capitalization and punctuation		✓	
Writes messages that can be understood by others		✓	
Shows understanding of sequence in writing		✓	
Stays on topic when writing			✓
Expresses original ideas	✓		
Elaborates with details			✓
Has an identifiable voice			✓
Chooses precise and vivid words		✓	
Takes risks with vocabulary			✓
Uses descriptive words	✓		
Writes in different forms			✓
Writes for different audiences and purposes			✓
Writes to record ideas and reflections	✓		
Other: Writes using rhyming words	✓		

© Pearson Education

Oral Language Behaviors Checklist ✓

What is it?	• A form to record your observations of children's speaking and listening behaviors at the beginning and throughout the year
What does it show?	• Children's facility with oral language • Children's ease at speaking and listening in various situations and for various purposes
How do I use it?	• Complete this form as you observe children speaking and listening, both individually and in groups. • Use your observations to assess children's needs and to make instructional decisions. • Attach the completed form to the Student Portfolio Sheet as additional information about the child.

A Checklist format is quick to complete and easy to interpret.

B Checklist includes all important aspects of a child's early oral language behaviors.

Teacher Form
Oral Language Behaviors Checklist ✓

Child Kristen Cleaver   **A**   Date 9/26

Behavior	Yes	No	Example
Follows simple oral directions	✓		
Follows directions of several steps		✓	got confused making a book page
Listens to stories read aloud	✓		
Participates actively when predictable rhymes and songs are read aloud	✓		
Understands and retells spoken messages	✓		
Gives precise directions		✓	couldn't explain how to get to office
Expresses ideas clearly	✓		
Responds appropriately to questions	✓		
Knows and uses many words	✓		
Participates in conversations and discussions	✓		
Listens in small-group situations	✓		
Listens in whole-group situations	✓		
Stays on topic in discussions		✓	led TV discussion away from topic
Uses conventional grammar and usage	✓		
Listens to others courteously, without interrupting	✓		
Can retell simple stories in sequence			forgot order in "Three Bears"
Recalls details from stories	✓		
Reads orally with appropriate fluency	✓		
Listens and speaks for various purposes	✓		
Adapts speaking to audience		✓	
Listens critically to oral readings, discussions, and messages	✓		
Connects cultural experiences and prior knowledge through speaking and listening	✓		
Other:			

Form for reproduction is on page 105.
Spanish form for reproduction is on page 131.

© Pearson Education

Survey
Profile of English Language Learners

What is it?
- A form to help identify the strengths and needs of children whose first language is not English

What does it show?
- A second-language learner's proficiency with spoken English and knowledge of basic English reading

How do I use it?
- Identify potential English language learners in the class.
- Observe children's behavior in classroom speaking and reading situations, and/or speak with children one on one.
- Use the criteria on the form to assess children's abilities.

What do I do next?

Consider one of these two options:

– Refer to the English Language Learners notes in the **Scott Foresman Reading Street** program teacher's edition, which offers modifications and extensions to help with many selections.

– Use the English Language Learners components of the program, which are aimed at developing skills for second-language learners as they read each program selection.

A Checklist format is easy to interpret.

B Space is provided for you to note your own responses.

Form for reproduction is on page 106.
Spanish form for reproduction is on page 132.

Teacher Form
Profile of English Language Learners

Child: Tomás Alvarez

Trait	Mostly	Unevenly	Rarely	Date/Comment
Speaks and/or understands a few basic words	✓			
Speaks fluently but makes frequent errors			✓	10/16 seems to know more words than he is comfortable using
Uses names of many objects		✓		
Uses and understands basic everyday vocabulary		✓		
Asks and answers simple questions			✓	10/16 reluctant to ask for help
Follows simple directions		✓		
Takes part in discussions			✓	10/16 good at communicating through art
Conveys ideas or stories through drawings	✓			
Needs pictures to comprehend simple text		✓		
Recognizes basic sound/letter relationships in words		✓		
Follows text being read aloud		✓		
Joins in choral reading	✓			10/16 likes to join in with the class
Retells predictable text		✓		

© Pearson Education

Myself as a Learner ✓

What is it?

- A survey that gives children an opportunity to tell you more about themselves
- A tool for getting children to reflect on their reading and writing

What does it show?

- Children's familiarity with books and print
- Children's exposure to print in the home

How do I use it?

- Read the questions to each child, or have children read and complete the form on their own. You may need to act as a scribe for some children.
- Attach the completed form to the Student Portfolio Sheet as additional information about the child.
- Consider using the form during parent conferences.

Child Form
Myself as a Learner ✓

Name **Kristen C.**   Date **Sept. 6**

	Yes	No	Comments
1. I like to listen to stories.	X		
2. I like to read books by myself.	X		
3. I know how to hold a book and turn the pages.	X		
4. I like to read out loud to others.	X		
5. I can figure out new words when I read.	X		
6. I like to write.	X		
7. I like to draw.	X		
8. I like to go to school.	X		
9. I read signs wherever I go.	X		

A Checklist format is easy to complete and interpret

B Comments space allows you to write down spontaneous remarks from the child or to have child elaborate.

Form for reproduction is on page 107.
Spanish form for reproduction is on page 133.

© Pearson Education

Survey
My Child as a Learner

What is it?

- A survey to help you get to know your students better from their families' perspective
- An opportunity to establish a positive relationship with your students' families from the start

What does it show?

- Children's behaviors that families observe at home
- Child-parent interactions with books and print
- A family's view of a child as a learner

How do I use it?

- Send the survey home at the beginning of the school year with a cover letter explaining the value of family input.
- Attach the completed form to the Student Portfolio Sheet as additional information about each child.
- Use it during parent conferences.

(A) Checklist format is quick to complete and easy to interpret.

(B) Comments provide information specific to each child in your class.

Form for reproduction is on page 108.
Spanish form for reproduction is on page 134.

Parent Form
My Child as a Learner

Child **Kristen Cleaver**   Parent/Guardian/Caregiver **Jeff Cleaver**   Date **10/21**

	Always	Sometimes	Never	Comments
1. My child asks to be read to.	**(A)**	✓		
2. My child can retell a book we have read or a television program we have watched.	✓			**(B)**
3. My child can predict what will happen next when reading a book or watching a television program.		✓		
4. My child picks up a book to read or look at alone.		✓		
5. My child reads or pretends to read at home.		✓		
6. My child knows how to hold a book, how to turn pages, and that print goes from left to right.	✓			
7. My child likes to write or pretend to write.		✓		writes some letters backwards—should we be concerned?
8. My child likes to talk about what he or she has written.		✓		
9. My child can follow an oral direction when given.		✓		
10. My child can follow a series of oral directions when given one time.		✓		
11. My child likes working with others.	✓			
12. My child tries to read words in the environment—signs, labels, logos.		✓		
13. My child likes to go to school.	✓			

© Pearson Education

Ongoing Teacher Observation

What is it?

- Observation that occurs in the context of teaching or classroom activities

- A way to check children's progress on a daily or weekly basis

- The basis for instructional decisions about individual children

How do I make observations?

- Choose one or more children to focus on each day.

- Select the literacy behavior, strategy, or skill that you wish to observe.

- Observe those children as they are participating in classroom activities.

- Using a clipboard, sticky note, customized form, or checklist, note a child's behavior or performance in the targeted skills.

- Include any comments, insights, or other information you regard as significant.

- Develop a record-keeping system that is convenient and informative for you.

Why should I record my observations?

- To remember information when you need to reflect on a child at the end of the day, week, grading period, or year

- As a helpful tool for presenting information to children, parents, and administrators

- For documentation when you need to explain why you've placed a child in a particular group or given a certain grade

- To plan strategies for intervening with children needing special attention

© Pearson Education

Running Record

What is it?

- An individually administered procedure of recording and analyzing a child's specific reading behaviors
- A method of deciding whether a text is at the appropriate instructional level for a child
- A means of determining the level of support a child will need while reading the material

What does it show?

- Teachers who administer regular running records gather evidence about the following:
  - reading strategies a child uses and how he or she uses them to derive meaning
  - decoding and word recognition strategies
  - comprehension of text
  - fluency and oral reading skills

When do I use it?

- As often as necessary to get a clear and ongoing picture of a child's precise reading behaviors (for example, at the beginning or end of a unit or grading period when you need to report progress to interested parties)

How do I use it?

- Use an excerpt from *Scott Foresman Reading Street,* from a trade book, or any other text that is at an appropriate reading level for the child.
- Make a photocopy for yourself of the passage you will have the child read.
- Observe the child closely as he or she reads aloud, and code behaviors on your copy of the text.
- Indicate the number of words per line, and note the miscues, or errors, that are made, as well as the strategies the child is using.
- Use the following notations and symbols:

© Pearson Education

- Accurate Reading (✓) – Record a check for each word read accurately.

- Substitutions – Draw a line through the text word and write the word substituted above the text word. If it is a nonsense word, write it phonetically.

- Self-correction (*sc*) – Write *sc* in a circle above the corrected word/text.

- Insertions (^) – Write the inserted word/phrase above the text word. Mark each insertion with a caret. Include any repetitions of words.

- Omissions – Circle the part(s) omitted.

- Hesitations – Underline and write *H* above the word the child hesitates over or has to be told.

- Mispronunciation/Misreading – Write the child's pronunciation of the word above the text word.

Name *Susan*   9/4/2009   (62)

What Is It?

H ✓ ✓ ✓ ✓ ✓ ✓ ✓ ✓ ✓ ✓ *water* ✓ ✓

Zhou likes to be near the ocean. He likes to hear the ~~waves~~. He likes   15

✓ ✓ ✓ ✓ ✓ ✓ ✓ ✓ ✓ ✓ ✓ *fly* ✓ ✓ ✓

to put his feet in (the) sand. He likes to see the birds^in the sky.   31

✓ ✓ ✓ ✓ (sc) ✓ ✓ ✓ ✓ ✓ ✓ ✓ ✓

One day, Zhou saw a little face in the water. The face was dark gray.   46

✓ ✓ ✓ ✓ ✓ ✓✓ ✓ ✓ ✓✓ ✓ ✓ ✓ ✓

The face had black eyes and a long nose like a dog. Zhou saw the face   62

growing ✓ ✓ ✓ ✓

going up and down in/the waves.   69

$$\frac{67 - 5}{67} = 93\%$$

© Pearson Education

$$\frac{\text{Total number of words read} - \text{number of errors}}{\text{Total number of words read}} = \text{percentage score}$$

Teacher Form
Retelling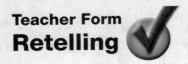

What is retelling?	• A post-reading recall of what children can remember from reading or listening to a particular text
	• An oral or written recounting of narrative or expository text in a child's own words
What does it show?	• Children's ability to understand narrative text elements and author's purpose, and to connect stories to personal experiences and other texts
	• Children's ability to understand expository text – the relationship of main ideas and details, organizational structure, author's purpose, and inferences – and to connect texts to personal experiences and prior knowledge (Moss 2004)
What does the research say?	• Several researchers have found that using retellings improves student understanding of text. (Gambrell, Koskinen, and Kapinus 1991; Gambrell, Pfeiffer, and Wilson 1985; Morrow 1986)
	• Pappas (1991) found that kindergarten children were just as capable of retelling informational text as narrative.
How do I do it?	• In preparation:
	– Have children attempt retelling narrative or expository text only after you have taught and modeled the procedure and they understand the task.
	– Have children practice in groups before retelling for assessment purposes.
	– Teach text structures (narrative and expository) separately to avoid confusing children.
	• For oral retellings, read the passage aloud to the child, or have the child read the selected text. Remind the child to remember everything he or she has heard or read. Then ask the child to tell you everything about what he or she read.

© Pearson Education

- For written retellings, read the text aloud to children, or ask them to read it silently. Remind the children to remember everything they can. Immediately after reading, have children write out what they remember about the text.

How do I use the Retelling Forms?

Record your scores and observations on either the narrative or the expository checklist. Try to record at least one narrative and one expository retelling from each child per unit.

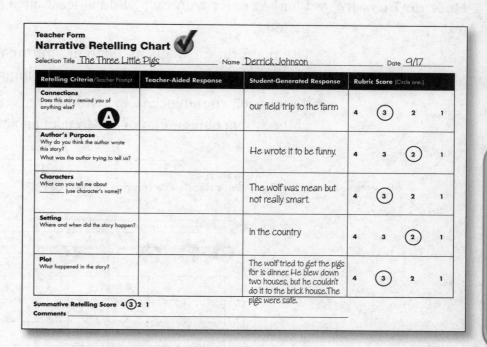

Teacher Form
Narrative Retelling Chart ✔

Selection Title _The Three Little Pigs_   Name _Derrick Johnson_   Date _9/17_

Retelling Criteria/Teacher Prompt	Teacher-Aided Response	Student-Generated Response	Rubric Score (Circle one.)
Connections Does this story remind you of anything else? **A**		our field trip to the farm	4 ③ 2 1
Author's Purpose Why do you think the author wrote this story? What was the author trying to tell us?		He wrote it to be funny.	4 3 ② 1
Characters What can you tell me about _____ (use character's name)?		The wolf was mean but not really smart.	4 ③ 2 1
Setting Where and when did the story happen?		in the country	4 3 ② 1
Plot What happened in the story?		The wolf tried to get the pigs for is dinner. He blew down two houses, but he couldn't do it to the brick house. The pigs were safe.	4 ③ 2 1

Summative Retelling Score 4 ③ 2 1
Comments _____

A Criteria reflect comprehension skills.

B Criteria help children pinpoint key information.

Teacher Form
Expository Retelling Chart ✔

Selection Title _Animal Babies_   Name _Derrick Johnson_   Date _10/2_

Retelling Criteria/Teacher Prompt	Teacher-Aided Response	Student-Generated Response	Rubric Score (Circle one.)
Connections Did this selection make you think about something else you have read? What did you learn about as you read this selection?	The Ugly Duckling	I learned the names of baby animals.	4 3 ② 1
Author's Purpose Why do you think the author wrote this selection?		to tell about animals and their babies	④ 3 2 1
Topic What was the selection mostly about?		what animal babies look like	4 ③ 2 1
Important Ideas What is important for me to know about _____ (topic)? **B**		Most animal babies need their mothers when they are young.	④ 3 2 1
Conclusions What did you learn from reading this selection?	what the babies look like and act like	the names of animal babies	④ 3 2 1

Summative Retelling Score 4 ③ 2 1
Comments _____

Forms for reproduction are on pages 109, 110. Spanish forms for reproduction are on pages 135, 136.

© Pearson Education

3 • Informal Assessment

Teacher Form
Work Habits Conference Record

What is it?	• A form to record results of teacher observations and child-teacher conversations about the child's work habits
What does it show?	• A child's progress toward working independently
How do I use it?	• Plan to confer with each child at least once per grading period.
	• Use the form for frequent, ongoing, informal conversations about the child's progress and areas for improvement.
	• Tailor each conference to the child's needs, interests, and abilities; encourage him or her to take an active role.

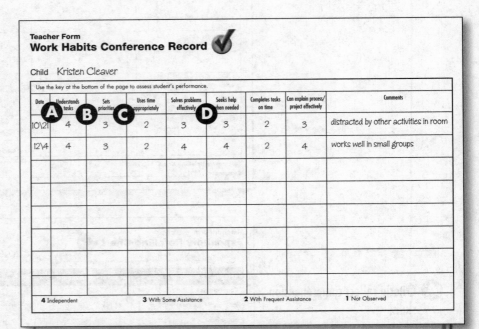

Teacher Form
Work Habits Conference Record

Child Kristen Cleaver

Use the key at the bottom of the page to assess student's performance.

Date	Understands tasks (A)	Sets priorities (B)	Uses time appropriately (C)	Solves problems effectively	Seeks help when needed (D)	Completes tasks on time	Can explain process/ project effectively	Comments
10\21	4	3	2	3	3	2	3	distracted by other activities in room
12\4	4	3	2	4	4	2	4	works well in small groups

4 Independent   **3** With Some Assistance   **2** With Frequent Assistance   **1** Not Observed

A Did the child understand the assignment's purpose and procedures? Did he or she follow directions?

B Was the child able to decide which parts of the assignment had to be done first?

C Did the child allot time appropriately and use the time productively?

D Did the child know when it was time to seek help? Did he or she seek out the right resources (books, peers, teacher, and so on)?

Form for reproduction is on page 111.
Spanish form for reproduction is on page 137.

© Pearson Education

Teacher Form
Skills Conference Record

What is it?
- A means of focusing and recording results of child-teacher conversations about the child's reading, writing, speaking, and listening

What does it show?
- A child's reading, writing, speaking, and listening behaviors and strategies

How do I use it?
- Use the checklist to summarize a student's progress or to help you transfer information to a more traditional reporting form

A Specific criteria in each area show particular strengths and needs.

B Comments can be made to record child's behavior or a specific concern.

C Checklist covers the continuum of child's skill growth.

Form for reproduction is on page 112.
Spanish form for reproduction is on page 138.

© Pearson Education

Teacher Form
Skills Conference Record

Grade 1

Child Marisol Lopez.   Teacher Ms. Rossi

		Proficient	Developing	Emerging	Not showing trait
Reading Comments:	Sets own purpose for reading		✓		
	Predicts and asks questions		✓		
	Retells/ summarizes	✓			
	Reads fluently		✓		
	Understands key ideas in a text		✓		
	Uses decoding strategies		✓		
	Makes text connections		✓		
	Other:				
Writing Comments:	Follows writing process		✓		
	Develops main idea and supporting details			✓	
	Organization of ideas			✓	
	Uses transitions			✓	
	Word choice expresses ideas			✓	
	Grammar and mechanics		✓		
	Other:				
Speaking and Listening Comments: Listens with interest to others	Follows instructions				
	Asks questions		✓		
	Answers questions		✓		
	Paraphrases		✓		
	Discussions		✓		
	Eye contact with audience		✓		
	Other:				

Teacher Form
Observing English Language Learners

What is it?
- A form to record your ongoing observations about how English language learners process what they read

What does it show?
- How English language learners use strategies to make sense of materials they read
- Children's growth and development in processing what they read

How do I use it?
- Use the form with second graders or with first graders in the second half of the year.
- Work with children individually as they read a new selection.
- Record your observations about how children deal with new words and concepts.
- Continue to review and record children's behaviors periodically as needed.
- Consider using the information in parent conferences.

A Behaviors identify common strategies for success in reading a new language.

B Space is provided to record children's development over time.

Teacher Form
Observing English Language Learners

Child: Tomás Alvarez

Behaviors Observed	Date: 10/27			Date: 11/18			Date:			Date:		
The child	Yes	No	Sometimes	Yes	No	Sometimes	Yes	No	Sometimes	Yes	No	Sometimes
• uses context clues to figure out new words		✓				✓						
• uses prior knowledge to figure out new words			✓	✓								
• uses visuals to decipher meaning	✓			✓								
• uses strategies to decipher meaning		✓				✓						
• can identify the strategies he or she is using		✓				✓						
• understands why he or she is using a particular strategy		✓		✓								
• assesses his or her own progress			✓	✓								
• generally understands what the class is reading		✓				✓						

General Comments

10/27: need to work harder on strategies with Tomás

11/18: Tomás doing much better at drawing on prior knowledge. Is beginning to see the logic of strategies.

Form for reproduction is on page 113.
Spanish form for reproduction is on page 139.

© Pearson Education

Observing My Child's Reading

What is it?	• A form to allow parents to evaluate and comment on their child's reading
	• A way to keep parents knowledgeable about and involved in their child's reading progress
What does it show?	• Reading behaviors parents noticed as their child read aloud to them
How do parents use it?	• Give copies of the form to parents during a conference or other meeting.
	• Ask parents to use the forms every few weeks to note their responses as their child reads aloud to them.
	• Encourage parents to comment on any other noteworthy aspects of their child's reading progress.

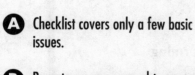 **A** Checklist covers only a few basic issues.

B Parents are encouraged to comment on any aspect of child's reading that they've noticed or are concerned about.

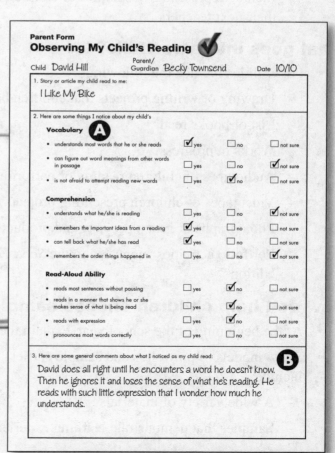

Form for reproduction is on page 114.
Spanish form for reproduction is on page 140.

© Pearson Education

Student Portfolios

What is a portfolio?

- A teacher-guided process in which children collect representative samples of their own reading, writing, speaking, and listening as a means of demonstrating growth over time

- A method of documenting growth by using the actual products children create during normal day-to-day learning

- A way to encourage children to feel ownership of their learning

What is the purpose of a portfolio?

- Portfolios may do any or all of the following:

  - Demonstrate children's growth and progress

  - Show children's strengths and needs

  - Help you make instructional decisions for children

  - Encourage children to assess their own growth and progress and to set new goals

  - Make it possible to share evidence of children's growth during family conferences

  - Include representative samples of children's work that you can pass along to their next teachers

What goes into a portfolio?

- Possibilities include the following:

  - Drawing or writing projects that children have done at school or at home

  - List of books read

  - Works in progress

  - Audiotapes of children reading or performing

  - Videotapes of children presenting projects or performing

  - Photographs of group projects and products

  - Portfolio activities suggested in the *Scott Foresman Reading Street* teacher's edition

How do I help children choose samples for their portfolios?

- At the beginning of the school year, explain the process of developing a portfolio.

- Show models of portfolios and sample entries. Explain that portfolios should include:

  - A wide variety of materials

  - Samples that demonstrate learning experiences

© Pearson Education

- Pieces that show growth or improvement over time
- Materials that indicate that children have challenged themselves to try something different

- Periodically set aside time for children to examine their work and think about which pieces they would like to include in their portfolios.
  - Ask children to complete an entry slip that can be attached to each piece of work selected for inclusion in the portfolio.
  - The entry slip can be a blank piece of paper, a sticky note, or brief form designed for this purpose.
  - Ask children to briefly describe the work sample, the rationale for including it, and a reflection on the quality of the work, for example, *What I Chose, Why I Chose It,* and *What I Like About It.*

- Encourage children to include other documentation of literacy growth and progress, such as journal entries, inventories, writing drafts and revised copies, reading and writing logs, and peer assessments of portfolio work.

How do I involve the family in the portfolio process?

- At the beginning of the year, send home a letter to parents informing them about portfolios.

- Share children's portfolios during parent conferences as children explain the contents, how projects were developed, and how portfolio pieces were selected.

- While viewing portfolios with parents, point out children's strengths and progress over time.

What can I do at the end of each grading period?

- Hold portfolio conferences toward the end of each grading period to help children reflect on the contents of their portfolios.

- Have children decide which pieces to take home, which pieces remain in the portfolio, and which pieces to lend to you to update their Student Portfolio Sheets.

What can I do at the end of the school year?

- Hold final conferences with children to help them reflect on their portfolios and decide what to save and what to eliminate.

- Have children decide what to take home and what to pass along to their next teachers, for example, the pieces they are most proud of or the ones that show the most growth.

© Pearson Education

Child Form
Reading Log

| What is it? | • A form to help children keep track of the literature they have read |
| | • An opportunity for children to tell what they like about each piece of literature |

| What does it show? | • How children evaluate what they read |

| How do children use it? | • Children may list either materials from the reading program or pieces of literature they have selected on their own. |
| | • Children may put this form in their portfolios as a way of documenting what they have read. |

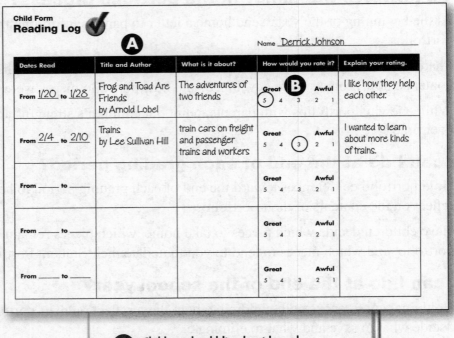

A Children should list the title and authors of selections they have read.

B Have children circle the rating they would give each selection. Children should give a reason or two to explain or support their ratings.

Form for reproduction is on page 115.
Spanish form for reproduction is on page 141.

© Pearson Education

Writing Log ✓

What is it?

- A form to help children keep track of the pieces they have written

- An opportunity for children to look over their writing pieces and assess their writing growth over time

What does it show?

- How children evaluate their own writing

How do children use it?

- Children may put this form in their portfolios as a way of keeping track of what they have written.

Child Form
Writing Log ✓

Child _Taylor F._   Date _10/30_

Teacher _Ms Rossi_   Grade _2_

Date	Title **A**	Type of writing	How I felt about this piece	What I liked or disliked	Put in portfolio
Oct 15	Silly Friends		④ 3 2 1	the funny parts	✓
Oct 27	My Halloween Costume		4 ③ 2 1	the surprise at the end	
			4 3 2 1		
			4 3 2 1		
			4 3 2 1		
			4 3 2 1		

B (over "What I liked or disliked")

Key
4 = Excellent
3 = Good
2 = Fair
1 = Poor

A If children haven't titled a piece yet, they can use a working title such as "My Puppy" or "Mystery Story."

B Encourage children to assess their own writing and to point out the strengths of the piece.

Form for reproduction is on page 116.
Spanish form for reproduction is on page 142.

© Pearson Education

Child Form
Peer Assessment

What is it?

- A form that allows children to assess their peers' portfolio work
- An opportunity to help children become aware of and value different points of view

What does it show?

- How children evaluate one or more pieces in a classmate's portfolio

How do children use it?

- Ask children to assess their peers' work at least once per grading period.
- Have children keep this form in their portfolios, and encourage them to use it during peer conferences.
- If you feel that children need more space to write, reproduce this form on larger paper.

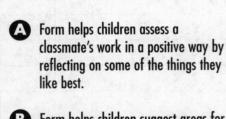

A Form helps children assess a classmate's work in a positive way by reflecting on some of the things they like best.

B Form helps children suggest areas for improvement.

C Form allows children to make suggestions that the classmate might not have considered.

Form for reproduction is on page 117.
Spanish form for reproduction is on page 143.

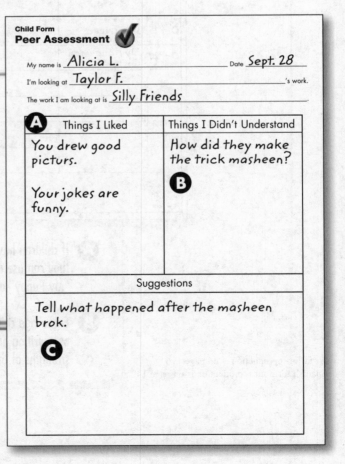

Child Form
Peer Assessment

My name is _Alicia L._ Date _Sept. 28_
I'm looking at _Taylor F._ 's work.
The work I am looking at is _Silly Friends_

A Things I Liked	Things I Didn't Understand
You drew good pictures.	How did they make the trick masheen?
Your jokes are funny.	**B**
Suggestions	
Tell what happened after the masheen brok. **C**	

© Pearson Education

Teacher Form
Portfolio Guide ✓

What is it?
- A form for managing the contents of a child's portfolio, whether teacher or child selected
- A cover sheet showing the portfolio contents at-a-glance

What does it show?
- An overall composite of a child's strengths and needs, interests, and attitudes throughout the year
- A child's selected work throughout the year

How do I use it?
- Track forms and work submitted at various times during the year.
- Fill in dates as a reminder of when to collect additional submissions.

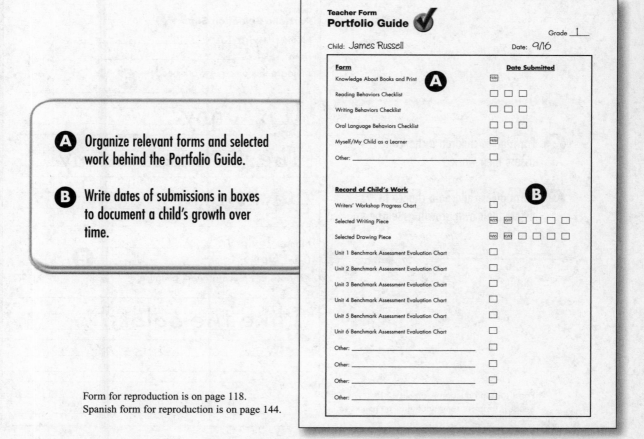

A Organize relevant forms and selected work behind the Portfolio Guide.

B Write dates of submissions in boxes to document a child's growth over time.

Form for reproduction is on page 118.
Spanish form for reproduction is on page 144.

© Pearson Education

Child Form
Portfolio Selection Slips

What is it?	• A form to help children choose the pieces to include in their portfolios
	• An opportunity for children to think about what they have included in their portfolios
What does it show?	• A child's rationale for including each piece
	• What children think of their work
How do children use it?	• Allow children to look over their work, decide whether they wish to submit it to their portfolio, and complete the form.
	• Attach slip to the child's work and place in portfolio for future review of contents.

A Form gives children a chance to assess their work.

B Form gives children a chance to assess their own growth as learners.

Child Form
Portfolio Selection Slips
Name _Taylor F._
Date _Oct. 3_
I choose this piece of work because **A**

It is funny.
The pictures are my
best work.

Name _Taylor F._
Date _Oct. 3_ **B**
I choose this piece of work because

I like the colors.

Form for reproduction is on page 119.
Spanish form for reproduction is on page 145.

© Pearson Education

Teacher Summary Reports

What are they?

- Forms that teachers can compile as a way of summarizing and assessing a child's reading, writing, speaking, and listening growth over time

What do they show?

- A child's reading, writing, speaking, and listening behaviors and strategies

How do I use them?

- In order to document a child's progress, compile and synthesize the information from any or all these assessment types and forms:
  - Ongoing Teacher Observations
  - Running Records
  - Retellings
  - Conference Records
  - Observing English Language Learners
  - Reading Log
  - Writing Log
  - Peer Assessment
  - Portfolio Guide
- Use what you've gathered when you prepare grades or as you get ready for conferences with children, parents, administrators, or resource teachers.

© Pearson Education

Early Literacy Behaviors Checklist

What is it?
- a cumulative list of major skills, behaviors, and concepts covered in kindergarten and first grade
- a place to compile information collected from various teacher observations and child performances

What does it show?
- where a child is in his or her growth as a reader and language user
- specific information about the following:
  - ✓ the child's level of comfort with books and print
  - ✓ the child's oral language development
  - ✓ the child as a speaker and listener
  - ✓ the child as a reader
  - ✓ the child as a writer

How do I use it?
- Whenever a summary of a child's progress is required, compile the information from your various assessment tools onto this form.
- You can use this checklist at parent-teacher conferences, at grading periods, or at any other time a detailed yet concise report is needed.
- Some teachers also choose to use this checklist as an inventory of where the child is at the beginning of the school year.

© Pearson Education

Teacher Form
Early Literacy Behaviors Checklist

Name __Hiro Watanabe__

Date __9/10__   Grade __1__

A = Always
S = Sometimes
N = Never

Dates of Observations

Concepts of Print	9/10	11/15					
recognizes environmental print	A						
knows how to hold a book	A						
knows the parts of a book (front cover, back cover)	A						
distinguishes between title, author, and illustrator	A						
turns pages in sequence from front to back	A						
understands that print represents spoken language and conveys meaning	A						
knows the difference between letters and words	A						
tracks print from left to right and top to bottom	A						
knows that letters make up words	A						
matches spoken to written words	S						
Phonological/Phonemic Awareness							
identifies rhyming words	A						
produces rhyming words	S						
knows that words are made up of syllables	A						
isolates phonemes	S						
identifies initial phonemes in words	S						
identifies final phonemes in words	S						
segments and blends phonemes in words	S						
Phonics and Decoding							
identifies letters of the alphabet, both uppercase and lowercase	A						
recognizes own name in print	A						
connects sound to letter—consonants	S						
connects sound to letter—vowels	S						
uses letter-sound knowledge to read words	S						
uses context and picture clues to help identify words	S						

(A)

Teacher Form
Early Literacy Behaviors Checklist (continued)

Name __Hiro Watanabe__

Date __9/10__   Grade __1__

A = Always
S = Sometimes
N = Never

(B)

Dates of Observations

Comprehension	9/10	11/15					
retells stories with story structure, including setting, characters, and plot	S						
uses illustrations to understand stories	A						
predicts what will happen next	S						
connects concepts from literature to own life	S						
can identify genres of children's literature	S						
asks appropriate questions and makes appropriate comments about text and pictures	S						
infers and evaluates ideas and feelings	S						
demonstrates an understanding of thematic concepts	S						
Writing							
writes own name—first and last	A						
is moving from scribble writing to random letters and letter strings	A						
uses knowledge of letter sounds to write words	S						
understands the correspondence between spoken and written words in dictation when recording thoughts	A						
writes for a variety of purposes	S						
writes in a variety of genres: narrative, exposition, and poetry	S						
Speaking and Listening							
speaks in complete sentences	S						
engages freely in conversation in varied situations	S						
attends to others while they are speaking	S						
discriminates sounds appropriately	S						
pronounces sounds appropriately for age and language background	S						
uses increasingly complex oral language that is appropriate for age and language background	S						
follows oral directions	A						

A Specific information gives a clear picture of the child's growth

B Multiple observations allow you to track a child's literacy development

Forms for reproduction are on pages 120–121.
Spanish forms for reproduction are on pages 146–147.

© Pearson Education

3 • Informal Assessment

Teacher Form
Reading Strategy Assessment

What is it?
- A form to use at the end of each grading period to help you synthesize the information you've gathered about a child's reading progress

What does it show?
- A child's reading growth and progress over the course of a grading period
- A child's knowledge and use of reading strategies, including self-assessment

How do I use it?
- Use the checklist to summarize a child's progress or to help you transfer information to a more traditional reporting form.

A Criteria help you synthesize the information you've compiled from any of the forms and checklists you used throughout the grading period.

Form for reproduction is on page 122.
Spanish form for reproduction is on page 148.

Teacher Form
Reading Strategy Assessment ✓

Child __Taylor Finch__ Date __11/22__
Teacher __Ms. Rossi__ Grade __2__

		Proficient	Developing	Emerging	Not Showing Yet
Building Background Comments:	Previews		✓		
	Ask questions		✓		
	Predicts **A**		✓		
	Activates prior knowledge	✓			
	Sets own purposes for reading	✓			
	Other:				
Comprehension Comments: *Needs to slow down to improve comprehension.*	Retells/Summarizes		✓		
	Questions, evaluates ideas		✓		
	Paraphrases				✓
	Rereads/reads ahead for meaning			✓	
	Visualizes	✓			
	Uses decoding strategies		✓		
	Uses vocabulary strategies		✓		
	Understands key ideas of a text		✓		
	Other:				
Fluency Comments:	Adjusts reading rate		✓		
	Reads for accuracy		✓		
	Uses expression			✓	
	Other:				
Connections Comments:	Relates text to self		✓		
	Relates text to text			✓	
	Relates text to world		✓		
	Other:				
Self-Assessment Comments: *Works well in small groups.*	Is aware of: Strengths		✓		
	Needs		✓		
	Improvement/Achievement		✓		
	Sets and implements learning goals		✓		
	Maintains logs, records, portfolio				
	Works with others	✓			
	Shares ideas and materials	✓			
	Other:				

© Pearson Education

Writing Strategy Assessment ✓

What is it?

- A form to use at the end of each grading period to help you synthesize the information you've gathered about a second grader's writing progress

What does it show?

- A child's writing growth and progress over the course of a grading period based on the 6-Trait Writing System

- A child's knowledge and use of writing strategies, including self-assessment

How do I use it?

- Use the checklist to summarize a child's progress or to help you transfer information to a more traditional reporting form.

Form for reproduction is on page 123.
Spanish form for reproduction is on page 149.

A Criteria help you synthesize the information you've compiled from any of the forms and checklists you used throughout the grading period.

Teacher Form
Writing Strategy Assessment ✓

Child Taylor Finch   Date 11/22
Teacher Ms. Rossi   Grade 2

		Proficient	Developing	Emerging	Not showing trait
Ideas Comments:	Identifies purpose in opening paragraph		✓		
	States main idea		✓		
	Details support main idea		✓		
	Gathers ideas and information **A**		✓		
	Conclusion reinforces main idea			✓	
	Other:				
Organization Comments:	Product of writing process			✓	
	Has a clear beginning, middle, and end		✓		
	Begins with a topic sentence		✓	✓	
	Uses transitions between sentences and paragraphs				
	Uses order words (first, then, after, finally)		✓		
	Other:				
Voice Comments:	Speaks directly to audience			✓	
	Voice matches writer's purpose			✓	
	Shows rather than tells			✓	
	Writer's feelings and personality emerge		✓		
	Keeps reader's attention				
	Other:				
Word Choice Comments:	Uses vivid words to elaborate ideas		✓		
	Avoids slang and jargon		✓		
	Uses strong images or figurative language			✓	
	Uses action verbs versus linking verbs		✓		
	Uses new words to express ideas				
	Other:				
Sentence Fluency Comments:	Expresses thoughts in lively, varied sentences		✓		
	Mixes short and long sentences		✓		
	Includes questions, commands, and exclamations				
	Sentences flow logically from one to another		✓		
	Avoids choppy and wordy sentences		✓		
	Other:				
Conventions Comments:	Subjects and verbs are in agreement		✓		
	Uses correct punctuation for grade level	✓			
	Capitalizes proper nouns and sentence beginnings	✓			
	Forms plurals of nouns		✓		
	Words are spelled correctly		✓		
	Other:				

© Pearson Education

3 • Informal Assessment

Cumulative Folder Form

What is it?
- A cumulative record of a child's reading progress, to be placed in the child's permanent record that follows a child from year to year

What does it show?
- The most basic and permanent information on how the student performed during a school year, namely, scores for the Baseline Test, Unit Benchmark Tests, and End-of-Year Benchmark Test, the group in which the child received instruction, and any additional comments a teacher wants to make

How do I use it?
- Record scores and comments from unit to unit.
- Place the form into the child's cumulative folder at the end of the school year.

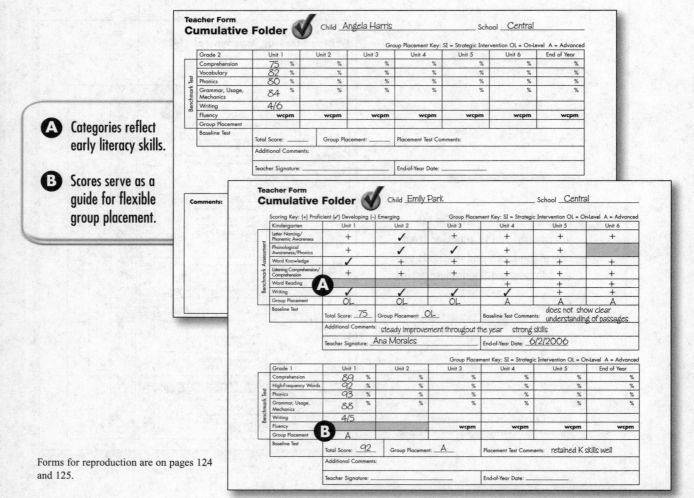

A Categories reflect early literacy skills.

B Scores serve as a guide for flexible group placement.

Forms for reproduction are on pages 124 and 125.

© Pearson Education

Chapter 4

Assessment of English Language Learners

Overview

What are the unique challenges in assessing English language learners?

- Many English language learners may quickly master *social* English, the conversational language skills and conventions used in everyday interactions with classmates.

- These same children frequently encounter difficulty with the *academic* English found on formal assessments.

- The structure of academic English is complex (e.g., spelling, word structure, inflected endings, fiction and nonfiction text structures, paragraph organization, and syntax).

- The vocabulary of academic English consists of specialized meanings of common words, abstract concepts and multiple-meaning words, and words based on Latin and Greek roots. (Bielenberg 2004/2005)

- The topics and concepts of comprehension passages are frequently unfamiliar, and children may not understand the purposes of assessment tasks divorced from real-life contexts.

- Formal assessments often fail to reflect the diverse cultural and linguistic experiences of English language learners, and then have limited value for helping teachers select appropriate instructional strategies. (Garcia 1994)

How are *Scott Foresman Reading Street* assessments sensitive to the needs of English language learners?

- Both formal and informal classroom-based *Scott Foresman Reading Street* assessments help teachers monitor growth in the basic reading and expression skills of alphabetic understanding, decoding, sight vocabulary, and grammar, along with measurement of the more complex skills of fluency, comprehension, and vocabulary.

- Reading comprehension test passages reflect diverse ethnic and cultural experiences.

- Texts are matched to the age, interest, and background knowledge of the children.

- Most assessment tasks are embedded in contexts with which children have familiarity. The comprehension assessments are generally based on themes and topics explored in instruction; vocabulary is assessed within the context of the passage; and writing tasks relate to main ideas of the texts.

- Visual cues, pictures, and other non-print features accompany assessment passages.

- The language of the test directions and assessment items is straightforward and unambiguous.

© Pearson Education

What instructional strategies will help prepare my English language learners for formal assessments?

- Pre-teach the "language of tests" encountered in directions and test items, including:

  - Question words: *who, what, which, where, when, why,* and *how*

  - Emphasis words: *not, except, most likely, probably, major, both, neither, either, most,* and *least*

  - Action words: *tell, read, answer, mark,* and *find*

- Teach use of context clues to interpret meaning of unfamiliar terms.

- Highlight and discuss routinely the *academic* language, vocabulary, syntax, and narrative and expository text structures encountered in textbooks and trade books.

- Coach children in oral and written retelling, so they develop a "sense" of text types, features, conventions, and organization. English language learners, like most primary-grade children, relate to the concrete nature of informational text, and expository retellings familiarize them with the common text structures, such as sequence, description, classification, compare/contrast, cause/effect, and problem/solution. In addition, retelling is an important first step to summarization, a critical skill for success in literacy.

- Provide regular opportunities for meaningful oral language experiences in which English language learners participate in discussion of important topics and perform the activities required on tests, such as reading, answering, describing, and stating and supporting opinions. Encourage them to use vocabulary that will support academic language development.

- Download and examine released forms of state and standardized assessments, reviewing the various item constructions and test vocabulary. Model and discuss the thinking steps involved in responding to both multiple-choice and constructed-response items.

- Read aloud, think aloud, and model the purposeful and strategic behaviors of effective readers.

- Provide repeated opportunities for practicing all the techniques above.

What accommodations are appropriate to use with the *Scott Foresman Reading Street* formal assessments?

- Accommodating the needs of English language learners ensures fairness and full participation in the formal assessments. A general rule of thumb is to use the same accommodations in testing situations as used in instruction. For instance, if children receive part of their instruction in their native language, then it is appropriate to translate test directions and comprehension questions into the student's first language.

© Pearson Education

- Acceptable accommodations might include:
  - providing additional testing time and allowing frequent or extended breaks
  - administering the tests at times most beneficial to the children
  - administering the tests in small groups or in one-on-one settings
  - reading test directions to students in English (or in the students' native languages, if this is feasible), and repeating as often as needed
  - simplifying the language and sentence structure of test directions
  - requesting that children restate and clarify test directions in their own words
  - discussing the pictures and any graphics, such as maps, to ensure that children can interpret them
  - allowing the use of bilingual word-for-word translation dictionaries
  - reading test passages orally to children in English, and repeating as often as necessary, when listening comprehension is being assessed, as in Kindergarten and Grade 1
  - reading comprehension questions orally to children in English or in their native languages
  - allowing children to respond orally to questions or dictate answers for transcription
- In providing accommodations to children, it is important not to compromise the intent of the assessment. It is never appropriate to read the reading comprehension *passages* or the vocabulary and grammar questions to children in English or their native languages; nor is it allowable to transcribe children's oral responses to the writing prompts. These practices alter the constructs of the assessments. For example, the reading comprehension assessments are designed to measure both word recognition and understanding, so reading the selections to students actually changes the intent of the test.

What are the *best* ways to assess the strengths and needs of English language learners?

- Through informal and on-going classroom-based assessment, teachers can observe, monitor, and judge the quality of children's work.

- Multiple assessments mirror the learning process, while single assessments capture one moment at a time, much like the difference between a video or album of photographs and a single snapshot.

- Observing small, consistent increases in learning over time is most reliable. The goal is continuous improvement.

- Frequent monitoring addresses learning in progress, allows for correction of misconceptions as they occur, and provides helpful feedback to English language learners.

© Pearson Education

- Teaching children to assess their own reading progress helps to build independence in language and learning.

- Authentic assessment activities enhance, rather than diminish, instructional time, because they are part of instruction. Activities include classroom observation, language-experience stories, story telling or writing, tape recordings of oral reading, reading-response logs, and journals. (Garcia, 1994)

© Pearson Education

References

Bielenberg, B., and L. W. Fillmore. "The English They Need for the Test." *Educational Leadership*, vol. 62, no. 4 (December 2004/January 2005); pp. 45–49.

Garcia, G. E. "Assessing the Literacy Development of Second-Language Students: A Focus on Authentic Assessment." In *Kids Come in All Languages: Reading Instruction for ESL Students*. Ed. Spangenberg-Urbshat, K., and R. Pritchard, pp. 180–205. Newark, DE: International Reading Association, 1994.

Lenters, K. "No Half Measures: Reading Instruction for Young Second-Language Learners." *The Reading Teacher*, vol. 58, no. 4 (December 2004/January 2005); pp. 328–336.

Moss, B. "Teaching Expository Text Structures Through Information Trade Book Retellings." *The Reading Teacher*, vol. 57, no. 8 (May 2004); pp. 710–718.

Zwiers, J. "The Third Language of Academic English." *Educational Leadership*, vol. 62, no. 4 (December 2004/January 2005); pp. 60–63.

© Pearson Education

Teacher Form
Profile of English Language Learners

What is it?

- A form to help identify the strengths and needs of students whose first language is not English

What does it show?

- A second-language learner's proficiency with speaking, reading, and writing English

How do I use it?

- Identify students whose English proficiency you are uncertain about.
- Compile samples of the students as they speak, read aloud, and write.
- Use the criteria on the form to assess students' abilities in the various language areas.
- Use the form as a rough guideline of where students are and where they may need help.

What do I do next?

- Refer to the English Language Learners notes in the *Scott Foresman Reading Street* program teacher's edition, which offers modifications and extensions to help with many selections.
- Use the English Language Learners components of the program, which are aimed at developing skills for second-language learners as they read each program selection.

A Checklist format is easy to interpret.

B Space is provided for you to note your own responses.

Form for reproduction is on page 106.
Spanish form for reproduction is on page 132.

Teacher Form
Profile of English Language Learners

Child: Tomás Alvarez

Trait	Mostly	Unevenly	Rarely	Date/Comment
Speaks and/or understands a few basic words	✓			
Speaks fluently but makes frequent errors			✓	10/16 seems to know more words than he is comfortable using
Uses names of many objects		✓		
Uses and understands basic everyday vocabulary		✓		
Asks and answers simple questions			✓	10/16 reluctant to ask for help
Follows simple directions		✓		
Takes part in discussions			✓	10/16 good at communicating through art
Conveys ideas or stories through drawings	✓			
Needs pictures to comprehend simple text		✓		
Recognizes basic sound/letter relationships in words		✓		
Follows text being read aloud		✓		
Joins in choral reading	✓			10/16 likes to join in with the class
Retells predictable text		✓		

© Pearson Education

Observing English Language Learners

What is it?	• A form to record your ongoing observations about how English language learners process what they read
What does it show?	• How English language learners use strategies to make sense of materials they read • Students' growth and development in processing what they read
How do I use it?	• Work with students individually as they read a new selection. • Record your observations about how students deal with new words and concepts. • Continue to review and record students' behaviors periodically as needed. • Consider using the information on the form in parent conferences.

A Behaviors identify common strategies for success in reading a new language.

B Space is provided to record children's development over time.

Teacher Form
Observing English Language Learners ✓

Child: Tomás Alvarez

Behaviors Observed — **A** — **B**

The child	Date: 10/27 Yes	No	Sometimes	Date: 11/18 Yes	No	Sometimes	Date: Yes	No	Sometimes	Date: Yes	No	Sometimes
• uses context clues to figure out new words		✓				✓						
• uses prior knowledge to figure out new words			✓	✓								
• uses visuals to decipher meaning	✓			✓								
• uses strategies to decipher meaning		✓				✓						
• can identify the strategies he or she is using		✓				✓						
• understands why he or she is using a particular strategy		✓		✓								
• assesses his or her own progress			✓	✓								
• generally understands what the class is reading			✓	✓				✓				

General Comments

10/27: need to work harder on srategies with Tomás

11/18: Tomás doing much better at drawing on prior knowledge. Is beginning to see the logic of strategies.

Form for reproduction is on page 113.
Spanish form for reproduction is on page 139.

© Pearson Education

4 • ELL Assessment

Chapter 5 **Grading**

Overview

What are the purposes of grading?

- The primary goals are to:
  - Support learning and to encourage children's success
  - Inform children, parents, teachers, and others about children's achievement of standards
- Many experts also suggest that a fair grading system can also serve as an effective technique for motivation. (Guskey, 2002)

How do the terms "evaluation," "score," and "grade" differ?

- **Evaluation** is the assignment of value to the evidence of learning provided by the child through formative or summative assessments.

- A **score** or **mark** is the evaluative number or label given on any single test or assignment.

- A **grade** is the number or letter reported at the end of an instructional period as a summary statement of a child's performance. A grade may be based on multiple scores.

What are some general guidelines for grading?

- Academic achievement is the major factor on which grades should be based. It is appropriate to provide feedback to children on their effort, behavior, ability, and attendance, but these factors should be documented and reported separately. (Marzano, 2000)

- Grades should communicate achievement of clear and public learning targets or standards. (O'Connor, 2002)

- Expectations for grading should be discussed with children at the beginning of instruction. Explain what you value and how you want learning demonstrated. Show models of children's work at different points in grade and score. Hold to your process!

- Grades alone are not always helpful, but grades accompanied by honest and descriptive feedback can provide incentives for increasing learning effort. (Afflerbach, 1993)

© Pearson Education

What are some opportunities for grading in *Scott Foresman Reading Street*?

- The program offers you opportunities to grade children's work on a variety of activities, including:
  - Daily classwork
  - Individual or group activities and projects
  - Writing assignments
  - Pages from the Practice Book
  - Pages from Fresh Reads for Differentiated Test Practice
  - Speeches and other oral presentations
  - Drawings or other artwork
  - Weekly Selection Tests
  - Unit Benchmark Tests
  - End-of-Year Benchmark Tests

What tools are available to make grading easier?

- The following features can all facilitate grading:
  - The teacher's edition includes scoring guides to help you determine grades for children's compositions.
  - Unit Benchmark Tests are accompanied by suggestions on how to convert raw scores into grades.
  - The Creating a Rubric form lets you create your own criteria and grading scales for other kinds of assignments.

Why are rubrics effective grading guides?

- Rubrics allow you to grade fairly, because the evidence for grading (strengths and weaknesses) is clearly specified for children and parents.
- Rubric criteria must be aligned with learning targets and standards.
- Rubrics are "coaching tools" that guide children in revising their work and improving learning.

Must all work be graded?

> "Any decision of consequence deserves more than one piece of evidence."
>
> (Pearson 1998)

- It is not mandatory, nor beneficial for children, to grade every piece of work. Summative assessments should be graded because they measure achievement of learning targets. When you grade formative assessments designed to monitor learning, you're actually grading how fast students achieve the standards. For example, you may want to assign certain Practice Book pages simply to help children better understand concepts, not to assign grades.

© Pearson Education

Is any grading system or scale recommended?

- Dividing a child's score on an assignment or test by the total possible score is one common way of determining a grade. What percentage score equals an A, B, or C, however, may vary widely from school to school. You should follow your school's or district's recommendations.

How important is it to have a school-wide or district-wide grading policy in place?

- It is very important to have an agreed-upon system to ensure that grading practices are consistently applied within the building and the district. If your school district does not have a general policy for converting scores to grades, or if the existing one is ambiguous or timeworn, you might propose that a group be convened for a period of time to study common issues related to grading and reporting. The resources listed in the bibliography for this chapter provide a good starting point.

References

Afflerbach, P. "Report Cards and Reading." *The Reading Teacher*, vol. 46, no. 6 (March 1993); pp. 458–465.

Guskey, T. R. *How's My Kid Doing?: A Parent's Guide to Grades, Marks, and Report Cards*. San Francisco, CA: Jossey-Bass, 2003.

Marzano, R. J. *Transforming Classroom Grading*. Alexandria, VA: Association for Supervision and Curriculum Development, 2000.

O'Connor, K. *How to Grade for Learning: Linking Grades to Standards*. Arlington Heights, IL: Skylight Professional Development, 2002.

Pearson, P. D. "Instruction and Assessment: Synergistic Energies or a Dysfunctional Family?" Presented at University of California, Berkeley, March 23, 1998.

© Pearson Education

Creating a Rubric ✓

What is it?	• A form that may be used for assessment of reading, writing, speaking, listening, or viewing assignments
	• A tool that allows you to focus assessment on the key concepts you emphasized during instruction
What does it show?	• How well a child exhibits his or her understanding of the key features of the assignment
	• Areas in which the child may require additional instruction
How do I use it?	• Choose the assessment criteria most relevant to a particular assignment. List them in the Features column.
	• Rate and comment on those features as you evaluate the assignment.
	• See the three forms that follow for converting these ratings to grades.

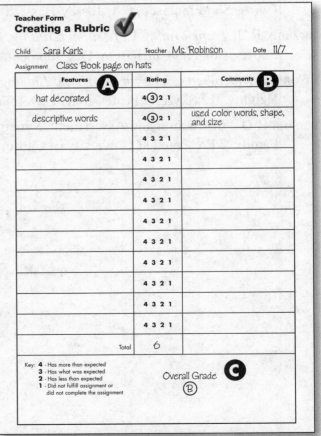

A The open-endedness of this form allows you to customize assessment features to meet the needs of every assignment.

B Your comments help you remember why you arrived at a rating and give you a starting point for discussing the assignment with the child or family.

C When desired, the rating may be turned into a letter grade.

Form for reproduction is on page 126.
Spanish form for reproduction is on page 150.

© Pearson Education

Grading Responses to Writing Prompts

- Writing prompts occur in several places in *Scott Foresman Reading Street*:
  - Following each selection and in the end-of-unit writing-process activity in the teacher's edition
  - In the Unit Benchmark Tests and the End-of-Year Benchmark Tests
- To grade children's writing, you can use the Creating a Rubric form. For your convenience, an example scale for a story has been completed for you below. Actual determinations about what score equals which grade will, however, vary with different teachers and districts.

A Decide which features of a story are important and list your own criteria.

B Comments help you remember why you arrived at a rating and give you a starting point for discussing the writing with the child.

C To determine the possible score, multiply the number of features by 4 (4 features x 4 = 16). Then add the ratings you've given the features to find the student's actual score. In this example 14 out of 16 = B.

Score	Grade
15–16	A
13–14	B
11–12	C
10	D
9 and below	F

Teacher Form
Creating a Rubric ✓

Child Jaime Novarro   Teacher Mr. Brownlee   Date 2/19

Assignment Narrative Writing

Features	Rating	Comments
The story is entertaining.	4 ③ 2 1	needs a little more punch
The story has a beginning, middle, and end.	④ 3 2 1	good sequence of events
The story has well-defined characters.	4 ③ 2 1	could use more description
The end ties the story together.	④ 3 2 1	surprise ending!
A	4 3 2 1	**B**
	4 3 2 1	
	4 3 2 1	
	4 3 2 1	
	4 3 2 1	
	4 3 2 1	
	4 3 2 1	
	4 3 2 1	
Total	14	

Key: **4** - Has more than expected
3 - Has what was expected
2 - Has less than expected
1 - Did not fulfill assignment or did not complete the assignment

C

Overall Grade ⓑ

Form for reproduction is on page 126.
Spanish form for reproduction is on page 150.

© Pearson Education

Grading Products and Activities

- The Creating a Rubric form lends itself to grading a variety of children's products and activities, including:
  - Class discussions
  - Speeches
  - Retellings
  - Oral readings and dramatizations
  - Drawings, sculptures, and other artwork
  - Graphic organizers such as Venn diagrams, story maps, concept maps, and K-W-L charts

- Two examples and grading scales – for an individual oral presentation and for a class discussion – are provided here. Actual determinations about what score equals which grade will, however, vary with different teachers and districts.

- In determining the criteria on which to evaluate children's work, you may find it helpful to refer to the various teacher summary reports described earlier or to the other checklists in this handbook.

© Pearson Education

(A) Example for an ORAL PRESENTATION

(B) To get a grade:
5 features x 4 = 20;
19 out of 20 = A.

Score	Grade
18–20	A
15–17	B
12–14	C
10–11	D
9 and below	F

Teacher Form
Creating a Rubric ✔️

Child Jake Simon   Teacher Ms. Jacks   Date 3/8

Assignment Story Retelling **(A)**

Features	Rating	Comments
practiced before presenting	④ 3 2 1	very smooth presentation
plot structure—beginning, middle, end	4 ③ 2 1	seemed to end several times
explained problem and solution	④ 3 2 1	clear and logical
used voice and facial expressions	④ 3 2 1	Great!
confidence in front of group	④ 3 2 1	Good improvement! seemed very calm
	4 3 2 1	
	4 3 2 1	
	4 3 2 1	
	4 3 2 1	
	4 3 2 1	
	4 3 2 1	
	4 3 2 1	
(B) Total	19	

Key: **4** - Has more than expected
3 - Has what was expected
2 - Has less than expected
1 - Did not fulfill assignment or did not complete the assignment

Overall Grade
(A)

(C) Example for a CLASS DISCUSSION

(D) To determine a grade:
4 features x 4 = 16;
14 out of 16 = B.

Score	Grade
15–16	A
13–14	B
11–12	C
10	D
9 and below	F

Form for reproduction is on page 126.
Spanish form for reproduction is on page 150.

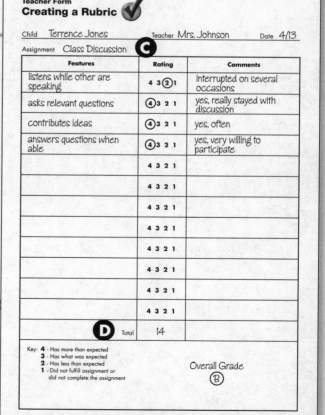

Teacher Form
Creating a Rubric ✔️

Child Terrence Jones   Teacher Mrs. Johnson   Date 4/13

Assignment Class Discussion **(C)**

Features	Rating	Comments
listens while other are speaking	4 3 ② 1	interrupted on several occasions
asks relevant questions	④ 3 2 1	yes, really stayed with discussion
contributes ideas	④ 3 2 1	yes, often
answers questions when able	④ 3 2 1	yes, very willing to participate
	4 3 2 1	
	4 3 2 1	
	4 3 2 1	
	4 3 2 1	
	4 3 2 1	
	4 3 2 1	
	4 3 2 1	
(D) Total	14	

Key: **4** - Has more than expected
3 - Has what was expected
2 - Has less than expected
1 - Did not fulfill assignment or did not complete the assignment

Overall Grade
(B)

© Pearson Education

Grading Group Activities

Grading Group Activities

- You can use the Creating a Rubric form to assign grades for group work. Children can be graded in one of two ways:

  – As group members working together

  – As individuals contributing to the group effort

- When evaluating the group as a unit, use criteria that emphasize children's ability to work together in an efficient and cooperative manner. Be mindful that cooperative or group grading can unfairly reward or penalize individual children.

- When assigning grades to individual children in a group, use criteria that emphasize the specific tasks the child must do. You may assign those tasks to children yourself, or, if they are able, children might choose tasks on their own.

- The examples provided here show ways to evaluate and grade groups as well as individual children within groups. Actual determinations about what score equals which grade will vary with different teachers and districts.

© Pearson Education

A Example for a COOPERATIVE GROUP ACTIVITY

B These criteria assess children's ability to work together cooperatively and effectively.

C To determine a group grade:
4 features x 4 = 16;
16 out of 16 = A.

Score	Grade
15–16	A
13–14	B
11–12	C
10	D
9 and below	F

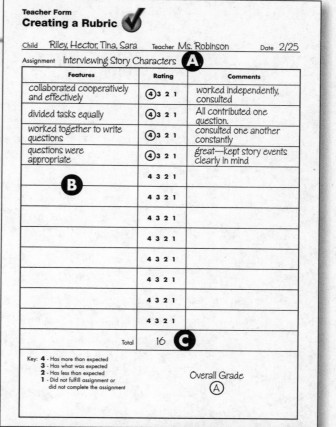

Teacher Form
Creating a Rubric ✔

Child Riley, Hector, Tina, Sara   Teacher Ms. Robinson   Date 2/25 **A**
Assignment Interviewing Story Characters **A**

Features	Rating	Comments
collaborated cooperatively and effectively	④ 3 2 1	worked independently, consulted
divided tasks equally	④ 3 2 1	All contributed one question.
worked together to write questions	④ 3 2 1	consulted one another constantly
questions were appropriate	④ 3 2 1	great—kept story events clearly in mind
B	4 3 2 1	
	4 3 2 1	
	4 3 2 1	
	4 3 2 1	
	4 3 2 1	
	4 3 2 1	
	4 3 2 1	
	4 3 2 1	
Total	16 **C**	

Key: **4** - Has more than expected
3 - Has what was expected
2 - Has less than expected
1 - Did not fulfill assignment or did not complete the assignment

Overall Grade
Ⓐ

D Example for an INDIVIDUAL IN A GROUP

E These criteria assess individual children according to the specific tasks they have performed.

F To determine a grade:
3 features x 4 = 12;
9 out of 12 = C.

Score	Grade
11–12	A
10	B
9	C
8	D
7 and below	F

Teacher Form
Creating a Rubric ✔

Child Riley Fox   Teacher Ms. Robinson   Date 2/25
Assignment Being/Interviewing Story Characters **D**

Features	Rating	Comments
understood character being portrayed.	④ 3 2 1	really understood Jesse Wilson well
acted in character during discussion	4 3 ② 1	sometimes did not stay in character
asked good questions of other characters	4 ③ 2 1	showed good understanding of story
E	4 3 2 1	
	4 3 2 1	
	4 3 2 1	
	4 3 2 1	
	4 3 2 1	
	4 3 2 1	
	4 3 2 1	
	4 3 2 1	
	4 3 2 1	
F Total	9	

Key: **4** - Has more than expected
3 - Has what was expected
2 - Has less than expected
1 - Did not fulfill assignment or did not complete the assignment

Overall Grade
Ⓒ

Form for reproduction is on page 126.
Spanish form for reproduction is on page 150.

© Pearson Education

Forms in English

© Pearson Education

Child

Date

Behavior	Yes	Not Yet	Comments
Knows how to hold book right side up			
Knows how to turn pages sequentially, front to back			
Knows that books have titles, authors, and illustrators			
Makes predictions from title, cover, and illustrations			
Can differentiate between pictures and text			
Knows that text and pictures relate to each other			
Tracks print from left to right and top to bottom			
Knows that print represents spoken words			
Knows that there are spaces between words			
Joins in reading text with a familiar, repetitive, or predictable pattern			
After multiple class readings, revisits the book, "reading" the story independently			
Other:			

© Pearson Education

Reading Behaviors Checklist ✔

Child

Date

Behavior	Yes	No	Not Applicable
Recognizes letters of the alphabet			
Recognizes name in print			
Recognizes some environmental print, such as signs and logos			
Knows the difference between letters and words			
Knows the difference between capital and lowercase letters			
Understands function of capitalization and punctuation			
Recognizes that book parts such as cover, title page, and table of contents offer information			
Recognizes that words are represented in writing by specific sequences of letters			
Recognizes words that rhyme			
Distinguishes rhyming and nonrhyming words			
Knows letter-sound correspondences			
Identifies and isolates initial sounds in words			
Identifies and isolates final sounds in words			
Blends sounds to make spoken words			
Segments one-syllable/two-syllable spoken words into individual phonemes			
Reads consonant blends and digraphs			
Reads and understands endings such as -es, -ed, -ing			
Reads vowels and vowel diphthongs			
Reads and understands possessives			
Reads and understands compound words			
Reads simple sentences			
Reads simple stories			
Understands simple story structure			
Other:			

© Pearson Education

Writing Behaviors Checklist

Child   Date

Behavior	Yes	No	Not Applicable
Produces detailed and relevant drawings			
Dictates messages for others to write			
Writes using scribble, drawing, or letterlike forms			
Distinguishes between writing and drawing			
Writes own name and other important words			
Writes all letters of the alphabet, capital and lowercase			
Writes labels or captions for illustrations and possessions			
Writes messages that move from left to right and top to bottom			
Uses phonological knowledge to map sounds to letters when writing			
Holds pencil and positions paper correctly			
Uses basic capitalization and punctuation			
Writes messages that can be understood by others			
Shows understanding of sequence in writing			
Stays on topic when writing			
Expresses original ideas			
Elaborates with details			
Has an identifiable voice			
Chooses precise and vivid words			
Takes risks with vocabulary			
Uses descriptive words			
Writes in different forms			
Writes for different audiences and purposes			
Writes to record ideas and reflections			
Other:			

© Pearson Education

Teacher Form
Oral Language Behaviors Checklist

Child

Date

Behavior	Yes	No	Example
Follows simple oral directions			
Follows directions of several steps			
Listens to stories read aloud			
Participates actively when predictable rhymes and songs are read aloud			
Understands and retells spoken messages			
Gives precise directions			
Expresses ideas clearly			
Responds appropriately to questions			
Knows and uses many words			
Participates in conversations and discussions			
Listens in small-group situations			
Listens in whole-group situations			
Stays on topic in discussions			
Uses conventional grammar and usage			
Listens to others courteously, without interrupting			
Can retell simple stories in sequence			
Recalls details from stories			
Reads orally with appropriate fluency			
Listens and speaks for various purposes			
Adapts speaking to audience			
Listens critically to oral readings, discussions, and messages			
Connects cultural experiences and prior knowledge through speaking and listening			
Other:			

© Pearson Education

Teacher Form

Profile of English Language Learners

Child: _____

Trait	Mostly	Unevenly	Rarely	Date/Comment
Speaks and/or understands a few basic words				
Speaks fluently but makes frequent errors				
Uses names of many objects				
Uses and understands basic everyday vocabulary				
Asks and answers simple questions				
Follows simple directions				
Takes part in discussions				
Conveys ideas or stories through drawings				
Needs pictures to comprehend simple text				
Recognizes basic sound/letter relationships in words				
Follows text being read aloud				
Joins in choral reading				
Retells predictable text				

© Pearson Education

Name _____   Date _____

	Yes	No	Comments
1. I like to listen to stories.			
2. I like to read books by myself.			
3. I know how to hold a book and turn the pages.			
4. I like to read out loud to others.			
5. I can figure out new words when I read.			
6. I like to write.			
7. I like to draw.			
8. I like to go to school.			
9. I read signs wherever I go.			

© Pearson Education

Parent Form
My Child as a Learner

Child

Parent/Guardian/
Caregiver

Date

	Always	Sometimes	Never	Comments
1. My child asks to be read to.				
2. My child can retell a book we have read or a television program we have watched.				
3. My child can predict what will happen next when reading a book or watching a television program.				
4. My child picks up a book to read or look at alone.				
5. My child reads or pretends to read at home.				
6. My child knows how to hold a book, how to turn pages, and that print goes from left to right.				
7. My child likes to write or pretend to write.				
8. My child likes to talk about what he or she has written.				
9. My child can follow an oral direction when given.				
10. My child can follow a series of oral directions when given one time.				
11. My child likes working with others.				
12. My child tries to read words in the environment—signs, labels, logos.				
13. My child likes to go to school.				

© Pearson Education

© Pearson Education

Teacher Form

Narrative Retelling Chart

Selection Title _____

Name _____ Date _____

Retelling Criteria/Teacher Prompt	Teacher-Aided Response	Student-Generated Response	Rubric Score (Circle one.)			
Connections Does this story remind you of anything else?			4	3	2	1
Author's Purpose Why do you think the author wrote this story? What was the author trying to tell us?			4	3	2	1
Characters What can you tell me about _____ (use character's name)?			4	3	2	1
Setting Where and when did the story happen?			4	3	2	1
Plot What happened in the story?			4	3	2	1

Summative Retelling Score 4 3 2 1

Comments _____

Teacher Form

Expository Retelling Chart

Selection Title _____ Name _____ Date _____

Retelling Criteria/Teacher Prompt	Teacher-Aided Response	Student-Generated Response	Rubric Score (Circle one.)
Connections Did this selection make you think about something else you have read? What did you learn about as you read this selection?			4 3 2 1
Author's Purpose Why do you think the author wrote this selection?			4 3 2 1
Topic What was the selection mostly about?			4 3 2 1
Important Ideas What is important for me to know about _____ (topic)?			4 3 2 1
Conclusions What did you learn from reading this selection?			4 3 2 1

Summative Retelling Score 4 3 2 1

Comments _____

© Pearson Education

© Pearson Education

Teacher Form

Work Habits Conference Record

Child _____

Use the key at the bottom of the page to assess student's performance.

Date	Understands tasks	Sets priorities	Uses time appropriately	Solves problems effectively	Seeks help when needed	Completes tasks on time	Can explain process/ project effectively	Comments

4 Independent　　**3** With Some Assistance　　**2** With Frequent Assistance　　**1** Not Observed

Skills Conference Record

Grade _____

Child _____   Teacher _____

		Proficient	Developing	Emerging	Not showing trait
Reading Comments:	Sets own purpose for reading	☐	☐	☐	☐
	Predicts and asks questions	☐	☐	☐	☐
	Retells/summarizes	☐	☐	☐	☐
	Reads fluently	☐	☐	☐	☐
	Understands key ideas in a text	☐	☐	☐	☐
	Uses decoding strategies	☐	☐	☐	☐
	Makes text connections	☐	☐	☐	☐
	Other:	☐	☐	☐	☐
Writing Comments:	Follows writing process	☐	☐	☐	☐
	Develops main idea and supporting details	☐	☐	☐	☐
	Organization of ideas	☐	☐	☐	☐
	Uses transitions	☐	☐	☐	☐
	Word choice expresses ideas	☐	☐	☐	☐
	Grammar and mechanics	☐	☐	☐	☐
	Other:	☐	☐	☐	☐
Speaking and Listening Comments:	Follows instructions	☐	☐	☐	☐
	Asks questions	☐	☐	☐	☐
	Answers questions	☐	☐	☐	☐
	Paraphrases	☐	☐	☐	☐
	Discussions	☐	☐	☐	☐
	Eye contact with audience	☐	☐	☐	☐
	Other:	☐	☐	☐	☐

© Pearson Education

© Pearson Education

Teacher Form

Observing English Language Learners

Child: _____

Behaviors Observed	Date:			Date:			Date:			Date:		
	Yes	No	Sometimes	Yes	No	Sometimes	Yes	No	Sometimes	Yes	No	Sometimes
The child												
• uses context clues to figure out new words												
• uses prior knowledge to figure out new words												
• uses visuals to decipher meaning												
• uses strategies to decipher meaning												
• can identify the strategies he or she is using												
• understands why he or she is using a particular strategy												
• assesses his or her own progress												
• generally understands what the class is reading												
General Comments												

Observing My Child's Reading
Parent/Guardian/Caregiver

Child   Date

---

1. Story or article my child read to me:

---

2. Here are some things I noticed about my child's

Vocabulary

- understands most words that he or she reads   ☐ yes   ☐ no   ☐ not sure

- can figure out word meanings from other words in passage   ☐ yes   ☐ no   ☐ not sure

- is not afraid to attempt reading new words   ☐ yes   ☐ no   ☐ not sure

Comprehension

- understands what he or she is reading   ☐ yes   ☐ no   ☐ not sure

- remembers the important ideas from a reading   ☐ yes   ☐ no   ☐ not sure

- can tell back what he or she has read   ☐ yes   ☐ no   ☐ not sure

- remembers the order things happened in   ☐ yes   ☐ no   ☐ not sure

Read-Aloud Ability

- reads most sentences without pausing   ☐ yes   ☐ no   ☐ not sure

- reads in a manner that shows he or she makes sense of what is being read   ☐ yes   ☐ no   ☐ not sure

- reads with expression   ☐ yes   ☐ no   ☐ not sure

- pronounces most words correctly   ☐ yes   ☐ no   ☐ not sure

---

3. Here are some general comments about what I noticed as my child read:

© Pearson Education

Observing My Child's Reading

© Pearson Education

Child Form
Reading Log

Name _____

Dates Read	Title and Author	What is it about?	How would you rate it?	Explain your rating.
From ____ to ____			**Great** 5 4 3 2 1 **Awful**	
From ____ to ____			**Great** 5 4 3 2 1 **Awful**	
From ____ to ____			**Great** 5 4 3 2 1 **Awful**	
From ____ to ____			**Great** 5 4 3 2 1 **Awful**	
From ____ to ____			**Great** 5 4 3 2 1 **Awful**	

Child Form
Writing Log

Child _____

Teacher _____

Date _____

Grade _____

Date	Title	Type of writing	How I felt about this piece	What I liked or disliked	Put in portfolio
			4 3 2 1		
			4 3 2 1		
			4 3 2 1		
			4 3 2 1		
			4 3 2 1		
			4 3 2 1		

Key
4 = Excellent
3 = Good
2 = Fair
1 = Poor

© Pearson Education

My name is _____ Date _____

I'm looking at _____'s work.

The work I am looking at is _____.

Things I Liked	Things I Didn't Understand

Suggestions

© Pearson Education

Child: _____   Date: _____

Form   **Date Submitted**

Knowledge About Books and Print   ☐

Reading Behaviors Checklist   ☐ ☐ ☐

Writing Behaviors Checklist   ☐ ☐ ☐

Oral Language Behaviors Checklist   ☐ ☐ ☐

Myself/My Child as a Learner   ☐

Other: _____   ☐

Record of Child's Work

Writers' Workshop Progress Chart   ☐

Selected Writing Piece   ☐ ☐ ☐ ☐ ☐ ☐

Selected Drawing Piece   ☐ ☐ ☐ ☐ ☐ ☐

Unit 1 Benchmark Assessment Evaluation Chart   ☐

Unit 2 Benchmark Assessment Evaluation Chart   ☐

Unit 3 Benchmark Assessment Evaluation Chart   ☐

Unit 4 Benchmark Assessment Evaluation Chart   ☐

Unit 5 Benchmark Assessment Evaluation Chart   ☐

Unit 6 Benchmark Assessment Evaluation Chart   ☐

Other: _____   ☐

Other: _____   ☐

Other: _____   ☐

Other: _____   ☐

© Pearson Education

Name _____

Date _____

I choose this piece of work because

_____

- -

_____

- -

_____

- -

✂ -

Name _____

Date _____

I choose this piece of work because

_____

- -

_____

- -

_____

- -

© Pearson Education

Early Literacy Behaviors Checklist

Name _____

Date _____ Grade _____

| A = Always |
| S = Sometimes |
| N = Never |

Dates of Observations

Concepts of Print						
recognizes environmental print						
knows how to hold a book						
knows the parts of a book (front cover, back cover)						
distinguishes between title, author, and illustrator						
turns pages in sequence from front to back						
understands that print represents spoken language and conveys meaning						
knows the difference between letters and words						
tracks print from left to right and top to bottom						
knows that letters make up words						
matches spoken to written words						
Phonological/Phonemic Awareness						
identifes rhyming words						
produces rhyming words						
knows that words are made up of syllables						
isolates phonemes						
identifies initial phonemes in words						
identifies final phonemes in words						
segments and blends phonemes in words						
Phonics and Decoding						
identifies letters of the alphabet, both uppercase and lowercase						
recognizes own name in print						
connects sound to letter—consonants						
connects sound to letter—vowels						
uses letter-sound knowledge to read words						
uses context and picture clues to help identify words						

© Pearson Education

Early Literacy Behaviors Checklist (continued)

Name _____

Date _____ Grade _____

A = Always
S = Sometimes
N = Never

Dates of Observations

Comprehension						
retells stories with story structure, including setting, characters, and plot						
uses illustrations to understand stories						
predicts what will happen next						
connects concepts from literature to own life						
can identify genres of children's literature						
asks appropriate questions and makes appropriate comments about text and pictures						
infers and evaluates ideas and feelings						
demonstrates an understanding of thematic concepts						
Writing						
writes own name—first and last						
is moving from scribble writing to random letters and letter strings						
uses knowledge of letter sounds to write words						
understands the correspondence between spoken and written words in dictation when recording thoughts						
writes for a variety of purposes						
writes in a variety of genres: narrative, exposition, and poetry						
Speaking and Listening						
speaks in complete sentences						
engages freely in conversation in varied situations						
attends to others while they are speaking						
discriminates sounds appropriately						
pronounces sounds appropriately for age and language background						
uses increasingly complex oral language that is appropriate for age and language background						
follows oral directions						

© Pearson Education

Reading Strategy Assessment

Child _____ Date _____

Teacher _____ Grade _____

	Proficient	Developing	Emerging	Not showing trait
Building Background				
Comments:				
Previews	☐	☐	☐	☐
Asks questions	☐	☐	☐	☐
Predicts	☐	☐	☐	☐
Activates prior knowledge	☐	☐	☐	☐
Sets own purposes for reading	☐	☐	☐	☐
Other:	☐	☐	☐	☐
Comprehension				
Comments:				
Retells/summarizes	☐	☐	☐	☐
Questions, evaluates ideas	☐	☐	☐	☐
Paraphrases	☐	☐	☐	☐
Rereads/reads ahead for meaning	☐	☐	☐	☐
Visualizes	☐	☐	☐	☐
Uses decoding strategies	☐	☐	☐	☐
Uses vocabulary strategies	☐	☐	☐	☐
Understands key ideas of a text	☐	☐	☐	☐
Other:	☐	☐	☐	☐
Fluency				
Comments:				
Adjusts reading rate	☐	☐	☐	☐
Reads for accuracy	☐	☐	☐	☐
Uses expression	☐	☐	☐	☐
Other:	☐	☐	☐	☐
Connections				
Comments:				
Relates text to self	☐	☐	☐	☐
Relates text to text	☐	☐	☐	☐
Relates text to world	☐	☐	☐	☐
Other:	☐	☐	☐	☐
Self-Assessment				
Comments:				
Is aware of: Strengths	☐	☐	☐	☐
Needs	☐	☐	☐	☐
Improvement/Achievement	☐	☐	☐	☐
Sets and implements learning goals	☐	☐	☐	☐
Maintains logs, records, portfolio	☐	☐	☐	☐
Works with others	☐	☐	☐	☐
Shares ideas and materials	☐	☐	☐	☐
Other:	☐	☐	☐	☐

© Pearson Education

Writing Strategy Assessment

Child _____ Date _____
Teacher _____ Grade _____

		Proficient	Developing	Emerging	Not showing trait
Ideas Comments:	Identifies purpose in opening paragraph	☐	☐	☐	☐
	States main idea	☐	☐	☐	☐
	Details support main idea	☐	☐	☐	☐
	Gathers ideas and information	☐	☐	☐	☐
	Conclusion reinforces main idea	☐	☐	☐	☐
	Other:	☐	☐	☐	☐
Organization Comments:	Product of writing process	☐	☐	☐	☐
	Has a clear beginning, middle, and end	☐	☐	☐	☐
	Begins with a topic sentence	☐	☐	☐	☐
	Uses transitions between sentences and paragraphs	☐	☐	☐	☐
	Uses order words (first, then, after, finally)	☐	☐		☐
	Other:	☐	☐	☐	☐
Voice Comments:	Speaks directly to audience	☐	☐	☐	☐
	Voice matches writer's purpose	☐	☐	☐	☐
	Shows rather than tells	☐	☐	☐	☐
	Writer's feelings and personality emerge	☐	☐	☐	☐
	Keeps reader's attention	☐	☐	☐	☐
	Other:	☐	☐		☐
Word Choice Comments:	Uses vivid words to elaborate ideas	☐	☐	☐	☐
	Avoids slang and jargon	☐	☐	☐	☐
	Uses strong images or figurative language	☐	☐	☐	☐
	Uses action verbs versus linking verbs	☐	☐	☐	☐
	Uses new words to express ideas	☐	☐	☐	☐
	Other:	☐	☐	☐	☐
Sentence Fluency Comments:	Expresses thoughts in lively, varied sentences	☐	☐	☐	☐
	Mixes short and long sentences	☐	☐	☐	☐
	Includes questions, commands, and exclamations	☐	☐		
	Sentences flow logically from one to another	☐	☐	☐	☐
	Avoids choppy and wordy sentences	☐	☐	☐	☐
	Other:	☐	☐	☐	☐
Conventions Comments:	Subjects and verbs are in agreement	☐	☐	☐	☐
	Uses correct punctuation for grade level	☐	☐	☐	☐
	Capitalizes proper nouns and sentence beginnings	☐	☐		
	Forms plurals of nouns	☐	☐	☐	☐
	Words are spelled correctly	☐	☐	☐	☐
	Other:	☐	☐	☐	☐

© Pearson Education

Teacher Form
Cumulative Folder

Child _____ School _____

Scoring Key: (+) Proficient (✓) Developing (−) Emerging

Group Placement Key: SI = Strategic Intervention OL = On-Level A = Advanced

Benchmark Assessment

Kindergarten	Unit 1	Unit 2	Unit 3	Unit 4	Unit 5	Unit 6
Letter Naming/ Phonemic Awareness						
Phonological Awareness/Phonics						
Word Knowledge						
Listening Comprehension/ Comprehension						
Word Reading						
Writing						
Group Placement						

Baseline Test _____ Group Placement: _____ Baseline Test Comments: _____

Total Score: _____ Group Placement: _____ End-of-Year Date: _____

Additional Comments: _____

Teacher Signature: _____

Group Placement Key: SI = Strategic Intervention OL = On-Level A = Advanced

Benchmark Test

Grade 1	Unit 1	Unit 2	Unit 3	Unit 4	Unit 5	End of Year
Comprehension	%	%	%	%	%	%
High-Frequency Words	%	%	%	%	%	%
Phonics	%	%	%	%	%	%
Grammar, Usage, Mechanics	%	%	%	%	%	%
Writing						
Fluency		wcpm	wcpm	wcpm	wcpm	wcpm
Group Placement						

Baseline Test _____ Group Placement: _____ Placement Test Comments: _____

Total Score: _____ Group Placement: _____ End-of-Year Date: _____

Additional Comments: _____

Teacher Signature: _____

© Pearson Education

© Pearson Education

Teacher Form
Cumulative Folder

 Child _____ School _____

Group Placement Key: SI = Strategic Intervention OL = On-level A = Advanced

Grade 2	Unit 1	Unit 2	Unit 3	Unit 4	Unit 5	Unit 6	End of Year
Comprehension	%	%	%	%	%	%	%
Vocabulary	%	%	%	%	%	%	%
Phonics	%	%	%	%	%	%	%
Grammar, Usage, Mechanics	%	%	%	%	%	%	%
Writing							
Fluency	wcpm	wcpm	wcpm	wcpm	wcpm	wcpm	wcpm
Group Placement							

(Benchmark Test)

Baseline Test

Total Score: _____ Group Placement: _____ Placement Test Comments:

Additional Comments:

Teacher Signature: _____ End-of-Year Date: _____

Comments:

Creating a Rubric

Child _____ Teacher _____ Date _____

Assignment _____

Features	Rating	Comments
	4 3 2 1	
	4 3 2 1	
	4 3 2 1	
	4 3 2 1	
	4 3 2 1	
	4 3 2 1	
	4 3 2 1	
	4 3 2 1	
	4 3 2 1	
	4 3 2 1	
	4 3 2 1	
	4 3 2 1	
Total		

Key: **4** - Has more than expected
3 - Has what was expected
2 - Has less than expected
1 - Did not fulfill assignment or
did not complete the assignment

© Pearson Education

Forms in Spanish

© Pearson Education

Nombre   Fecha

Comportamiento	Sí	Todavía no	Comentarios
Sabe sostener el libro correctamente			
Sabe pasar las páginas en secuencia, del principio al final			
Sabe que los libros tienen títulos, autores e ilustradores			
Hace inferencias a partir del título, la portada y las ilustraciones			
Sabe diferenciar entre las ilustraciones y el texto			
Sabe que el texto y las ilustraciones se relacionan entre sí			
Sigue el texto de izquierda a derecha y de arriba hacia abajo			
Sabe que las palabras escritas representan palabras del lenguaje oral			
Sabe que hay espacios en blanco entre las palabras			
Participa en la lectura en grupo de un texto con un patrón conocido, repetitivo o predecible			
Tras múltiples lecturas con la clase y el maestro, vuelve a tomar el libro, "leyendo" el cuento independientemente			
Otros:			

© Pearson Education

Formulario del maestro

Lista para evaluar el progreso en la lectura

Nombre   Fecha

Comportamiento	Sí	No	No aplica
Reconoce letras del alfabeto			
Reconoce su nombre escrito			
Reconoce algunas palabras escritas que encuentra en su ambiente, así como señales y logos			
Sabe la diferencia entre letras y palabras			
Sabe la diferencia entre letras mayúsculas y minúsculas			
Comprende la función de las mayúsculas y de la puntuación			
Reconoce que las distintas partes del libro, como la portada, la página del título y la tabla de contenido, ofrecen información			
Reconoce que las palabras son representadas en la escritura a través de secuencias específicas de letras			
Reconoce palabras que riman			
Distingue palabras que riman de palabras que no riman			
Conoce la correspondencia entre sonidos y letras			
Identifica y separa los sonidos iniciales de las palabras			
Identifica y separa los sonidos finales de las palabras			
Combina sonidos para formar palabras al hablar			
Separa palabras monosilábicas o de dos sílabas que escucha o habla en fonemas individuales			
Lee grupos consonánticos			
Lee y comprende terminaciones como -es, -ido, -ito			
Lee vocales y diptongos			
Lee y comprende los posesivos			
Lee y comprende palabras compuestas			
Lee oraciones sencillas			
Lee cuentos sencillos			
Comprende la estructura sencilla de un cuento			
Otros:			

© Pearson Education

Lista para evaluar el progreso en la escritura

Nombre   Fecha

Comportamiento	Sí	No	No aplica
Hace dibujos detallados y relevantes			
Dicta mensajes para que otros los escriban			
Escribe con garabatos, dibujos o formas parecidas a letras			
Distingue la escritura del dibujo			
Escribe su nombre y otras palabras importantes			
Escribe todas las letras del alfabeto, en mayúscula y minúscula			
Escribe rótulos o leyendas para dibujos y posesiones			
Escribe mensajes que van de izquierda a derecha y de arriba hacia abajo			
Usa conocimientos fonológicos para asociar sonidos con letras al escribir			
Sostiene el lápiz y coloca el papel correctamente			
Utiliza las reglas básicas de mayúsculas y de puntuación			
Escribe mensajes que los otros pueden entender			
Muestra comprensión de la secuencia al escribir			
Permanece en un tema al escribir			
Expresa ideas originales			
Elabora con detalles			
Es posible identificar su voz			
Elige palabras precisas y vívidas			
Se arriesga con el vocabulario			
Usa palabras descriptivas			
Escribe de maneras diferentes			
Escribe para públicos y propósitos diferentes			
Escribe para registrar ideas y reflexiones			
Otros:			

© Pearson Education

Lista para evaluar el progreso en el lenguaje oral

Nombre

Fecha

Comportamiento	Sí	No	Ejemplo
Sigue instrucciones orales sencillas			
Sigue instrucciones que contienen varios pasos			
Escucha cuentos que se le leen en voz alta			
Participa activamente cuando se leen en voz alta rimas y canciones predecibles			
Comprende y repite mensajes dichos en voz alta			
Da instrucciones precisas			
Expresa ideas claramente			
Responde a preguntas adecuadamente			
Sabe y emplea muchas palabras			
Participa en conversaciones y charlas			
Escucha cuando está en grupos pequeños			
Escucha cuando está con el grupo entero			
Mantiene la concentración en un tema durante las charlas			
Usa las normas gramaticales y de uso convencionales			
Escucha a los otros con cortesía, sin interrumpir			
Puede volver a contar cuentos sencillos siguiendo la secuencia			
Recuerda detalles de los cuentos			
Lee en voz alta con la fluidez adecuada			
Escucha y habla con propósitos diversos			
Adapta la forma de hablar al público			
Escucha críticamente lecturas realizadas en voz alta, conversaciones y mensajes			
Relaciona experiencias culturales y conocimientos anteriores cuando habla y escucha			
Otros:			

© Pearson Education

Formulario del maestro

Perfil de los estudiantes de inglés como segundo idioma

Niño:

Característica	Generalmente	De forma irregular	Raramente	Fecha/Comentario
Habla y/o entiende algunas palabras básicas				
Habla con fluidez pero comete errores frecuentemente				
Conoce y emplea los nombres de varios objetos				
Usa y entiende vocabulario diario básico				
Formula y responde a preguntas sencillas				
Sigue instrucciones sencillas				
Participa en charlas				
Expresa ideas o cuentos por medio de dibujos				
Necesita ilustraciones para entender un texto sencillo				
Reconoce la relación básica entre sonidos y letras en las palabras				
Sigue un texto que se le lee en voz alta				
Participa en la lectura en coro				
Vuelve a contar un texto predecible				

132

© Pearson Education

Nombre _____   Fecha _____

	Sí		
1. Me gusta escuchar cuentos que me leen.			
2. Me gusta leer cuentos yo solito/a.			
3. Sé sostener un libro y pasar las páginas.			
4. Me gusta leer en voz alta para otras personas.			
5. Puedo determinar el significado de palabras nuevas cuando leo.			
6. Me gusta escribir.			
7. Me gusta dibujar.			
8. Me gusta ir a la escuela.			
9. Leo las señales dondequiera que vaya.			

© Pearson Education

Mi hijo como estudiante ✓

Niño: Padres/Tutor: Fecha:

	Siempre	A veces	Nunca	Comentarios
1. Mi hijo pide que se le lean.				
2. Mi hijo puede volver a contar un libro que hemos leído o un programa de televisión que hemos visto.				
3. Mi hijo puede predecir lo que va a pasar cuando lee un libro o mira un programa de televisión.				
4. Mi hijo escoge un libro para leer o mirar solo.				
5. Mi hijo lee o hace que está leyendo en casa.				
6. Mi hijo sabe sostener un libro, darle vuelta a las páginas y que el texto va de izquierda a derecha.				
7. A mi hijo le gusta escribir o hacer que está escribiendo.				
8. A mi hijo le gusta hablar sobre lo que ha escrito.				
9. Mi hijo puede seguir unas instrucciones orales.				
10. Mi hijo puede seguir una serie de instrucciones orales cuando se dan a la vez.				
11. A mi hijo le gusta trabajar con otros.				
12. Mi hijo intenta leer palabras en su ambiente—señales, etiquetas, logos.				
13. A mi hijo le gusta ir a la escuela.				

© Pearson Education

© Pearson Education

Formulario del maestro

Tabla para volver a contar un texto narrativo

Título de la obra _____ Nombre _____ Fecha _____

Criterios para volver a contar/ Apunte del maestro	Respuesta con la ayuda del maestro	Respuesta del niño	Evaluación (Encierre uno en un círculo.)			
Conexiones ¿Te recuerda este cuento de algo?			4	3	2	1
La intención del autor ¿Por qué crees que el autor escribió este cuento? ¿Qué nos estaba intentando decir el autor?			4	3	2	1
Personajes ¿Qué me puedes decir de _____ (el nombre del personaje)?			4	3	2	1
Escenario ¿Dónde y cuándo tuvo lugar el cuento?			4	3	2	1
Argumento ¿Qué pasó en el cuento?			4	3	2	1

Evaluación acumulativa 4 3 2 1

Comentarios

135

Formulario del maestro

Tabla para volver a contar un texto expositivo

Título de la obra _____   Nombre _____   Fecha _____

Criterios para volver a contar/ Apunte del maestro	Respuesta con la ayuda del maestro	Respuesta del niño	Evaluación (Encierre uno en un círculo.)			
Conexiones ¿Esta obra te hizo pensar en otra cosa que has leído? ¿Qué has aprendido mientras leías esta obra?			4	3	2	1
La intención del autor ¿Por qué crees que el autor escribió esta obra			4	3	2	1
Tema ¿De qué se trataba en general esta obra?			4	3	2	1
Ideas importantes Para mí, ¿qué es importante saber sobre _____ (tema)?			4	3	2	1
Conclusiones ¿Qué aprendiste al leer esta obra?			4	3	2	1

Evaluación acumulativa 4 3 2 1

Comentarios _____

© Pearson Education

© Pearson Education

Formulario del maestro

Anotaciones de la conferencia sobre el rendimiento en los estudios

Nombre

Use la guía para calificar de la parte inferior de la página para evaluar el rendimiento del estudiante.

Fecha	Comprende las tareas	Establece prioridades	Emplea el tiempo adecuadamente	Resuelve los problemas eficazmente	Pide ayuda cuando la necesita	Termina las tareas a tiempo	Puede explicar el proceso/proyecto eficazmente	Comentarios

4 Independiente   **3** Con un poco ayuda   **2** Con ayuda frecuente   **1** No se observó

Anotaciones de la conferencia sobre el desarrollo del alfabetismo

Grado _____

Niño _____   Maestro _____

	competente	en vías de desarrollo	incipiente	No muestra la característica
Lectura Comentarios:				
Establece su propia razón para leer	☐	☐	☐	☐
Predice y hace preguntas	☐	☐	☐	☐
Vuelve a contar/Resume	☐	☐	☐	☐
Lee con fluidez	☐	☐	☐	☐
Comprende las ideas clave de un texto	☐	☐	☐	☐
Usa estrategias para descifrar	☐	☐	☐	☐
Hace conexiones con el texto	☐	☐	☐	☐
Otros:	☐	☐	☐	☐
Escritura Comentarios:				
Sigue el proceso de escribir	☐	☐	☐	☐
Desarrolla la idea principal y los detalles que la apoya	☐	☐	☐	☐
Organización de ideas	☐	☐	☐	☐
Usa transiciones	☐	☐	☐	☐
Las palabras escogidas expresan ideas	☐	☐	☐	☐
Gramática y ortografía y puntuación	☐	☐	☐	☐
Otros:				
Hablar y escuchar Comentarios:				
Sigue instrucciones	☐	☐	☐	☐
Hace preguntas	☐	☐	☐	☐
Contesta preguntas	☐	☐	☐	☐
Parafrasear	☐	☐	☐	☐
Hablar sobre temas	☐	☐	☐	☐
Mantiene contacto visual con el público	☐	☐	☐	☐
Otros:	☐	☐		☐

© Pearson Education

© Pearson Education

Formulario del maestro

Observar a los estudiantes de inglés como segundo idioma

Nombre:

Comportamientos observados	Fecha:			Fecha:			Fecha:			Fecha:		
	Sí	No	A veces	Sí	No	A veces	Sí	No	A veces	Sí	No	A veces
El estudiante												
• usa claves del contexto para figurarse y anticipar el significado de palabras nuevas												
• usa conocimientos previos para figurarse y anticipar el significado de palabras nuevas												
• usa recursos visuales para descifrar el significado												
• usa estrategias para descifrar el significado												
• sabe identificar las estrategias que usa												
• entiende por qué usa una estrategia en particular												
• evalúa su propio progreso												
• en general comprende lo que está leyendo la clase												

Comentarios generales

Observar la lectura de mi hijo

Nombre

Padre/
Tutor

Fecha

1. Cuento o artículo que mi hijo me ha leído:

2. Éstas son algunas cosas que observo en mi hijo relativas a

Vocabulario

- comprende la mayoría de las palabras que lee   ☐ sí   ☐ no   ☐ no estoy seguro/a

- puede determinar el significado de palabras a partir de otras palabras del pasaje   ☐ sí   ☐ no   ☐ no estoy seguro/a

- no teme leer palabras que nunca ha visto   ☐ sí   ☐ no   ☐ no estoy seguro/a

Comprensión

- comprende lo que lee   ☐ sí   ☐ no   ☐ no estoy seguro/a

- recuerda las ideas importantes   ☐ sí   ☐ no   ☐ no estoy seguro/a

- es capaz de repetir lo que ha leído   ☐ sí   ☐ no   ☐ no estoy seguro/a

- recuerda el orden en que ocurrieron las cosas   ☐ sí   ☐ no   ☐ no estoy seguro/a

Habilidad de lectura en voz alta

- lee la mayoría de las oraciones sin pausas   ☐ sí   ☐ no   ☐ no estoy seguro/a

- lee de forma tal que parece que ha entendido lo que ha leído   ☐ sí   ☐ no   ☐ no estoy seguro/a

- lee expresivamente   ☐ sí   ☐ no   ☐ no estoy seguro/a

- pronuncia la mayoría de las palabras correctamente   ☐ sí   ☐ no   ☐ no estoy seguro/a

3. A continuación incluyo algunos comentarios generales acerca de lo que he notado al escuchar leer al niño/a:

© Pearson Education

© Pearson Education

Formulario del niño
Diario de lectura

Nombre _____

Fechas leído	Título y autor	¿De qué se trata?	¿Cómo lo calificarías?	Explica tu calificación.
De ___ a ___			**Estupendo** **Terrible** 5 4 3 2 1	
De ___ a ___			**Estupendo** **Terrible** 5 4 3 2 1	
De ___ a ___			**Estupendo** **Terrible** 5 4 3 2 1	
De ___ a ___			**Estupendo** **Terrible** 5 4 3 2 1	
De ___ a ___			**Estupendo** **Terrible** 5 4 3 2 1	

Formulario del niño
Diario de escritura

Niño _____

Maestro _____

Fecha _____

Grado _____

Fecha	Título	Tipo de escritura	Lo que opiné de este trabajo	Lo que me gustó o no me gustó	En el portfolios
			4 3 2 1		
			4 3 2 1		
			4 3 2 1		
			4 3 2 1		
			4 3 2 1		
			4 3 2 1		

Clave
4 = Excelente
3 = Bueno
2 = Mediocre
1 = Pobre

© Pearson Education

Evaluación de los compañeros

Me llamo _____ Fecha _____

Estoy viendo el trabajo de _____.

El trabajo que estoy viendo se llama _____.

Cosas que me gustaron	Cosas que no entendí

Sugerencias

© Pearson Education

Guía de portafolios

Nombre _____ Fecha _____

Formulario

Fecha entregado

Conocimientos de libros y la palabra escrita ☐

Lista para evaluar el progreso en la lectura ☐ ☐ ☐

Lista para evaluar el progreso en la escritura ☐ ☐ ☐

Lista para evaluar el progreso en el languje oral ☐ ☐ ☐

Yo/Mi hijo como estudiante ☐

Otros: _____ ☐

Documentos sobre el trabajo del niño

Tabla de progreso del taller de escritores ☐

Trabajo escrito seleccionado ☐ ☐ ☐ ☐ ☐ ☐

Dibujo seleccionado ☐ ☐ ☐ ☐ ☐ ☐

Unidad 1 Tabla de evaluación para el examen de progreso ☐

Unidad 2 Tabla de evaluación para el examen de progreso ☐

Unidad 3 Tabla de evaluación para el examen de progreso ☐

Unidad 4 Tabla de evaluación para el examen de progreso ☐

Unidad 5 Tabla de evaluación para el examen de progreso ☐

Unidad 6 Tabla de evaluación para el examen de progreso ☐

Otros: _____ ☐

Otros: _____ ☐

Otros: _____ ☐

Otros: _____ ☐

© Pearson Education

Papelitos de selecciones para el portafolios

Nombre: _____

Fecha: _____

Escogí este trabajo porque

_____

_____

_____

_____

_____

_____

✂ ---

Nombre: _____

Fecha _____

Escogí este trabajo porque

_____

_____

_____

_____

_____

_____

© Pearson Education

Lista para evaluar el progreso en el alfabetismo ✓

Nombre _____

Fecha _____ Grado _____

S = Siempre
A = A veces
N = Nunca

Fechas de las observaciones

Conceptos de la palabra escrita						
reconoce la letra escrita en su ambiente						
sabe sostener un libro						
conoce las partes del libro (portada, contraportada)						
distingue entre el título, el autor y el ilustrador						
pasa las páginas en secuencia, del principio al final						
comprende que la letra escrita representa el lenguaje hablado y que imparte un significado						
sabe diferenciar entre letras y palabras						
sigue el texto de izquierda a derecha y de arriba hacia abajo						
sabe que las letras componen palabras						
empareja las palabras habladas con las escritas						
Fonología y fonemas						
identifica palabras que riman						
produce palabras que riman						
sabe que las palabras están compuestas de sílabas						
separa fonemas						
identifica fonemas iniciales en palabras						
identifica fonemas finales en palabras						
divide y combina fonemas en palabras						
Fonética y descifre						
identifica las letras del alfabeto, tanto mayúsculas como minúsculas						
reconoce su propio nombre escrito						
relaciona los sonidos con las letras—consonantes						
relaciona los sonidos con las letras—vocales						
usa conocimientos de letras y sonidos para leer palabras						
usa pistas del contexto y de las ilustraciones para identificar palabras						

© Pearson Education

Lista para evaluar el progreso en el alfabetismo
(continuación)

Nombre _____

Fecha _____ Grado _____

S = Siempre
A = A veces
N = Nunca

Fechas de las observaciones

Comprensión						
vuelve a contar cuentos con una organización adecuada, que incluye escenario, personajes y argumento						
usa ilustraciones para entender los cuentos						
predice lo que va a pasar						
relaciona los conceptos de la literatura con su propia vida						
puede identificar los diferentes géneros de la literatura infantil						
hace preguntas y comentarios adecuados sobre el texto y las ilustraciones						
infiere y evalúa ideas y sentimientos						
demuestra comprensión de los conceptos temáticos						
Escritura						
escribe su nombre y apellido						
progresa de escribir garabatos a letras sueltas y combinaciones de letras						
usa conocimientos de sondios y letras para escribir palabras						
comprende la correspondencia entre las palabras habladas y escritas en los dictados cuando emite pensamientos						
escribe para varios propósitos						
escribe una variedad de géneros: narraciones, exposiciones y poesía						
Hablar y escuchar						
habla con frases completas						
participa en conversaciones de varios temas						
presta atención a los demás mientras hablan						
discrimina los sonidos adecuadamente						
pronuncia los sonidos adecuadamente según su edad y conocimientos del idioma						
usa lenguaje que va aumentando en complejidad según su edad y conocimientos del idioma						
sigue instrucciones orales						

© Pearson Education

Evaluación de estrategias en la lectura

Niño _____ Fecha _____

Maestro _____ Grado _____

		Competente	En vías de desarrollo	Incipiente	No muestra la característica
Formación Comentarios:	Anticipa	☐	☐	☐	☐
	Hace preguntas	☐	☐	☐	☐
	Predice	☐	☐	☐	☐
	Utiliza conocimientos anteriores	☐	☐	☐	☐
	Establece sus propias razones para leer	☐	☐	☐	☐
	Otros:	☐	☐	☐	☐
Comprensión Comentarios:	Vuelve a contar/Resume	☐	☐	☐	☐
	Duda, evalúa ideas	☐	☐	☐	☐
	Parafrasea	☐	☐	☐	☐
	Lee otra vez/se adelanta en la lectura para captar el significado	☐	☐	☐	☐
	Visualiza	☐	☐	☐	☐
	Usa estrategias para descifrar	☐	☐	☐	☐
	Usa estrategias para vocabulario	☐	☐	☐	☐
	Comprende las ideas clave de un texto	☐	☐	☐	☐
	Otros:	☐	☐	☐	☐
Fluidez Comentarios:	Ajusta la velocidad con que lee	☐	☐	☐	☐
	Lee con precisión	☐	☐	☐	☐
	Es expresivo	☐	☐	☐	☐
	Otros:	☐	☐	☐	☐
Conexiones Comentarios:	Relaciona el texto con el texto	☐	☐	☐	☐
	Relaciona el texto consigo mismo	☐	☐	☐	☐
	Relaciona el texto con el mundo	☐	☐	☐	☐
	Otros:	☐	☐	☐	☐
Autoevaluación Comentarios:	Se da cuenta de: sus fuerzas	☐	☐	☐	☐
	sus necesidades	☐	☐	☐	☐
	su mejoría/sus logros	☐	☐		
	Establece y pone en práctica sus objetivos didácticos	☐	☐	☐	☐
	Mantiene diarios, documentos, portafolios	☐	☐	☐	☐
	Trabaja con otros	☐	☐	☐	☐
	Comparte ideas y materiales	☐	☐	☐	☐
	Otros:	☐	☐	☐	☐

© Pearson Education

Evaluación de estrategias en la escritura ✓

Niño _____ Fecha _____

Maestro _____ Grado _____

		Competente	En vías de desarrollo	Incipiente	No muestra la característica
Ideas Comentarios:	Identifica el propósito en el primer párrafo	☐	☐	☐	☐
	Expone la idea principal	☐	☐	☐	☐
	Los detalles apoyan la idea principal	☐	☐	☐	☐
	Junta ideas e información	☐	☐	☐	☐
	La conclusión reafirma la idea principal	☐	☐	☐	☐
	Otros:	☐	☐	☐	☐
Organización Comentarios:	Producto del proceso de escribir	☐	☐	☐	☐
	Tiene un principio, medio y final claros	☐	☐	☐	☐
	Comienza con una frase que expone la idea principal	☐	☐	☐	☐
	Usa transiciones entre las frases y los párrafos	☐	☐	☐	☐
	Usa palabras que muestran secuencia *(primero, luego, después, por fin)*	☐	☐	☐	☐
	Otros:	☐	☐	☐	☐
Voz Comentarios:	Habla directamente al público	☐	☐	☐	☐
	La voz corresponde al propósito del escritor	☐	☐	☐	☐
	Muestra en vez de contar	☐	☐	☐	☐
	Se notan los sentimientos y el carácter del escritor	☐	☐	☐	☐
	Mantiene la atención del lector	☐	☐	☐	☐
	Otros:	☐	☐	☐	☐
Selección de palabras Comentarios:	Usa palabras vivas para elaborar ideas	☐	☐	☐	☐
	Evita el argot y la jerga	☐	☐	☐	☐
	Usa imágenes fuertes o lenguaje figurativo	☐	☐	☐	☐
	Usa verbos activos, no copulativos	☐	☐	☐	☐
	Usa palabras nuevas para expresar ideas	☐	☐	☐	☐
	Otros:	☐	☐	☐	☐
Fluidez de frases Comentarios:	Expresa sus pensamientos con frases variadas y vivas	☐	☐	☐	☐
	Hay una mezcla de frases largas y cortas	☐	☐	☐	☐
	Incluye preguntas, mandatos y exclamaciones	☐	☐	☐	☐
	Las frases fluyen lógicmente entre sí	☐			
	Evita frases desonantes y de demasiadas palabras	☐	☐	☐	☐
	Otros:				
Normas Comentarios:	Los sujetos y los verbos concuerdan	☐	☐	☐	☐
	Usa correctamente la puntuación, según el grado	☐		☐	☐
	Usa letras mayúsculas para los sustantivos propios y la primera palabra de una frase	☐	☐	☐	☐
	Forma los plurales de los sustantivos	☐	☐	☐	☐
	La ortografía es correcta	☐	☐	☐	☐
	Otros:	☐	☐	☐	☐

© Pearson Education

Crear una guía para calificar

Nombre _____ Maestro _____ Fecha _____

Tarea

Características	Calificación	Comentarios
	4 3 2 1	
	4 3 2 1	
	4 3 2 1	
	4 3 2 1	
	4 3 2 1	
	4 3 2 1	
	4 3 2 1	
	4 3 2 1	
	4 3 2 1	
	4 3 2 1	
	4 3 2 1	
	4 3 2 1	
Total		

Guía: **4** - Más de lo esperado
3 - Lo que se esparaba
2 - Menos de lo esperado
1 - No realizó la tarea o no la terminó

Leído por: _____

© Pearson Education

Monitoring Progress Forms for Kindergarten
From *Scott Foresman Reading Street* Teacher's Editions

© Pearson Education

Unit 1 Literacy Development Checklist

	Unit 1	Unit 2	Unit 3	Unit 4	Unit 5	Unit 6
Concepts of Print						
• knows how to hold a book						
• knows the parts of a book (front cover, back cover)						
• knows the difference between letters and words						
• knows the difference between author and illustrator						
• tracks print from top to bottom and left to right						
• understands that print represents spoken language and conveys meaning						
• knows that letters make up words						
Phonological/Phonemic Awareness						
• can identify rhyming words						
• can produce rhyming words						
• knows that words are made up of syllables						
• knows that words are made up of letters						
• can isolate phonemes						
• can identify initial phonemes in words						
• can identify final phonemes in words						
• segments and blends phonemes in words						
Phonics and Decoding						
• identifies the letters of the alphabet, both upper- and lowercase						
• recognizes own name in print						
• can connect sound to letter—consonants						
• can connect sound to letter—vowels						
• uses letter-sound knowledge to read words						
Listening to Literature						
• retells stories with story structure, including setting, characters, and plot						
• uses illustrations to understand stories						
• predicts what will happen next						
• connects concepts from literature to own life						
Writing						
• writes own name—first and last						
• is moving from scribble writing to random letters and letter strings						
• uses knowledge of letter-sounds to write words						
• can dictate a story and "read" it back						

Key

+	Proficient
✓	Developing
–	Emerging

© Pearson Education

NAME THE LETTERS

Set A

A   D   C   E   B

e   b   a   d   c

D   a   B   C   E

NAME MORE LETTERS

Set B

D   a   b   e   C

c   d   B   a   e

A   e   D   b   c

READ THE WORDS

Set C

cat   dog   am

Note to Teacher Set A: Children name each letter. Set B: Children name more letters.
Set C: Children read words.

The Little School Bus

© Pearson Education

Note to Teacher Have children color the pictures that show characters from "Mary Had a Little Lamb."

© Pearson Education

FIND LETTERS

Set A

F   g   G   M   H

L   f   j   h   K

k   n   i   m   J

✂ - ✂

NAME LETTERS

Set B

M   K   g   J   n

m   h   N   i   H

k   j   f   I   L

✂ - ✂

READ THE WORDS

Set C

am   mom   I

Note to Teacher Set A: Children point to each letter named. Set B: Children name each letter.
Set C: Children read the words.

Fix-It Duck

© Pearson Education

SETTING

Note to Teacher Have children color the picture that shows where "Mr Spuffington Fixes It Himself" takes place.

© Pearson Education

NAME THE LETTERS

Set A

O r s P q

p o Q S R

s P O r q

✂ - ✂

NAME MORE LETTERS

Set B

R s p O q

e L S N m

r G o P k

✂ - ✂

READ THE WORDS

Set C

the   little   I

am

Note to Teacher Set A: Have children name the letters. Set B: Have children name each letter. Set C: Have children read each word.

Plaidypus Lost

© Pearson Education

Put the events from "The Three Little Kittens" in order.

Note to Teacher Have children cut out the pictures. Have them glue the pictures to another piece of paper in order to show what happened first, next, and last in "The Three Little Kittens."

© Pearson Education

NAME THE LETTERS

Set A

T	v	W	y	u
U	Y	x	z	t
Z	w	V	y	X

- -

NAME MORE LETTERS

Set B

T	Q	r	w	O
U	Y	v	R	x
t	y	W	Z	s

- -

READ THE WORDS

Set C

mom   dad   cat   dog

Note to Teacher Set A: Children name each letter. Set B: Children name each letter. *Miss Bindergarten Takes a Field Trip*
Set C: Children read words.

© Pearson Education

CLASSIFY AND CATEGORIZE

Sort these items into "tools" and "ingredients."

Note to Teacher Have children cut out the pictures and sort them into two groups: "Tools for Baking" and "Ingredients for Baking." Children should glue the groups of pictures onto another piece of paper.

© Pearson Education

IDENTIFY INITIAL /m/

Set A

DRAW /m/ WORDS

Set B

_____ _____ _____ _____

IDENTIFY MORE /m/ WORDS

Set C

man   a   cat

the   to

Note to Teacher Set A: Children listen for initial /m/. Set B: Children draw and label four /m/ pictures. Set C: Children read the words.

Julius

© Pearson Education

Cut out characters from "The Three Little Pigs."

Note to Teacher Have children cut out the characters from the story and glue them to another piece of paper. Have them draw a scene from the story using these characters.

© Pearson Education

IDENTIFY INITIAL *Tt*/t/ WORDS

© Pearson Education

Set A

IDENTIFY FINAL *Tt*/t/ WORDS

Set B

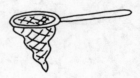

READ THE WORDS

Set C

mat	tap	Tim
top	cat	

Note to Teacher Set A: Children identify initial /t/. Set B: Children identify final /t/. Set C: Children read each word.

Dig Dig Digging

CLASSIFY AND CATEGORIZE

Note to Teacher Distribute another sheet of paper folded in half. Children write "Red" on one column and "Yellow" on the other. Cut out the objects and glue red objects under "Red" and yellow objects under "Yellow." Color the pictures red or yellow.

© Pearson Education

Day 5 Assessment Chart Unit 1

	Record Assessment Data		Calculate Weighted Score			Reteach ✓	Reassess
	Total Possible (Raw Score)	Child's Number Correct (Raw Score)		Child's Weighted Score	Total Possible (Weighted)		
Week 1 *The Little School Bus*							
A Letter Naming	15		÷3=		5		
B Letter Naming	15		÷3=		5		
C Read VC, CVC Words	3		=		3		
Week 2 *Fix-It Duck*							
A Letter Naming	15		÷3=		5		
B Letter Naming	15		÷3=		5		
C Read CVC Words	3		=		3		
Week 3 *Plaidypus Lost*							
A Letter Naming	15		÷3=		5		
B Letter Naming	15		÷3=		5		
C Read CVC Words	4		=		4		
Week 4 *Miss Bindergarten*							
A Letter Naming	15		÷3=		5		
B Letter Naming	15		÷3=		5		
C Read CVC Words	4		=		4		
Week 5 *Julius*							
A Identify Initial /m/	6		÷2=		3		
B Connect /m/ to *m*	6		÷2=		3		
C Read CVC Words	5		=		5		
Week 6 *Dig Dig Digging*							
A Identify Initial /t/	6		÷2=		3		
B Identify Final /t/	6		÷2=		3		
C Read CVC Words	5		=		5		
					76		

- **RECORD SCORES** In the Child's Number Correct column, record scores for the set(s) of the Day 5 Assessment used.

- **CALCULATE WEIGHTED SCORE** To calculate, divide by the number provided or simply enter the raw score if there is an equals sign (=).

- **RETEACH SKILLS** If a child is unable to successfully complete Sets A and/or B, then reteach the skills using the Reteach lessons on pp. DI•45–DI•50.

- **REASSESS** Use the same set of assessments or an easier set for reassessment.

© Pearson Education

IDENTIFY /a/

Set A

mat	at	top
am	met	Tam

 -

READ THE WORDS

Set B

Tam	at
mat	am

 -

READ THE SENTENCES

Set C

1. I have a mat.

2. I am Tam.

3. The mat is little.

4. Am I at the mat?

5. I am at the little mat.

Note to Teacher Set A: Children identify /a/ words. Set B: Children read each word.
Set C: Children read one or two sentences.

Life in an Ocean

© Pearson Education

COMPARE AND CONTRAST

Circle the two that are alike.

Put an X through the one that is different.

Note to Teacher Have children circle the two that are alike in the first line.
Have them put an *X* through the one that is different in the second line.

© Pearson Education

READ THE WORDS

Set A

mat   Sam   sat

READ MORE WORDS

Set B

at   mats   sat

Tam   am   mat

READ THE SENTENCES

Set C

1. The cat sat on the mat.

2. Is the cat on the mat?

3. I have a mat.

4. Sam is on the mat.

5. I have a little cat and a little mat.

Note to Teacher Set A: Children read each word. Set B: Children read each word.
Set C: Children read one or two sentences.

Armadillo's Orange

© Pearson Education

Draw where the story happens.
Then draw the animals.

© Pearson Education

Note to Teacher Have children draw where "The Mitten" takes place. Then have them draw the animals from the story.

READ THE WORDS

Set A

pat   map

Pam   tap

READ MORE WORDS

Set B

pass pats Pam

spat past taps

READ THE SENTENCES

Set C

1. My pet is a pig.

2. We have pink pants.

3. We have a little puppy.

4. Pam taps on the pad.

5. Pat got a big stamp.

Note to Teacher Set A: Children read each word. Set B: Children read each word. Set C: Children read one or two sentences.

Animal Babies in Grasslands

© Pearson Education

Color the picture that shows what
the story is about.

Note to Teacher Have children color the picture that shows what "All Night Near the Water" is all about.

© Pearson Education

READ THE WORDS

Set A

cat   cap   Cam   pat

READ MORE WORDS

Set B

caps   cat   past

cast   map   Cam

READ THE SENTENCES

Set C

1. The cats can nap.

2. Cam is my little cat.

3. We can have a cat.

4. Did Pat like the cap?

5. Dad can have the top.

Note to Teacher Set A: Children read each word. Set B: Children read each word.
Set C: Children read one or two sentences.

Bear Snores On

© Pearson Education

REALISM AND FANTASY

Color the make-believe bear.

© Pearson Education

READ THE WORDS

sip   tip

Tim   sit

READ MORE WORDS

sips   mist   Tim

tips   sits   mitt

READ THE SENTENCES

1. Tip is a cat.

2. We like my little cat.

3. Pam can sip it.

4. He can pass the cap.

5. It is for Tip.

Note to Teacher Set A: Children read each word. Set B: Children read each word.
Set C: Children read one or two sentences.

A Bed for the Winter

© Pearson Education

SEQUENCE

Put these events from "Willy's Winter Rest" in order.

Note to Teacher Have children cut out the three scenes and glue them to another sheet of paper in the correct order.

© Pearson Education

READ THE WORDS

Set A

sip   tip   Tim

pit

READ MORE WORDS

Set B

tips   mitt   pits

spit   sips   Tim

READ THE SENTENCES

Set C

1. I like the maps.

2. I have a cap for Tim.

3. He likes the cat.

4. Tim tips the cap.

5. I have a mat for my little cat.

Note to Teacher Set A: Children read each word. Set B: Children read each word.
Set C: Children read one or two sentences.

Whose Garden Is It?

© Pearson Education

REAL OR MAKE-BELIEVE

Color the make-believe pictures. Circle the real pictures.

Note to Teacher Have children color the pictures that are make-believe and circle the pictures that are real.

© Pearson Education

Day 5 Assessment Chart

Unit 2

	Record Assessment Data			Calculate Weighted Score		Reteach ✓	Reassess
	Total Possible (Raw Score)	Child's Number Correct (Raw Score)		Child's Weighted Score	Total Possible (Weighted)		
Week 1 *Life in an Ocean*							
A Identify /a/	6		÷2=		3		
B Read the Words	4		=		4		
C Read the Sentences	5		=		5		
Week 2 *Armadillo's Orange*							
A Read the Words	3		=		3		
B Read More Words	6		÷2=		3		
C Read the Sentences	5		=		5		
Week 3 *Animal Babies in Grasslands*							
A Read the Words	4		=		4		
B Read More Words	6		=		6		
C Read the Sentences	5		=		5		
Week 4 *Bear Snores On*							
A Read the Words	4		=		4		
B Read More Words	6		=		6		
C Read the Sentences	5		=		5		
Week 5 *A Bed for the Winter*							
A Read the Words	4		=		4		
B Read More Words	6		=		6		
C Read the Sentences	5		=		5		
Week 6 *Whose Garden Is It?*							
A Read the Words	4		=		4		
B Read More Words	6		=		6		
C Read the Sentences	5		=		5		
					83		

- **RECORD SCORES** In the Child's Number Correct column, record scores for the set(s) of the Day 5 Assessment used.
- **CALCULATE WEIGHTED SCORE** To calculate, divide by the number provided or simply enter the raw score if there is an equals sign (=).
- **RETEACH SKILLS** If a child is unable to successfully complete Sets A and/or B, then reteach the skills using the Reteach lessons on pp. DI·45–DI·50.
- **REASSESS** Use the same set of assessments or an easier set for reassessment.

© Pearson Education

READ THE WORDS

Set A

can   cab   bat   Nan

READ MORE WORDS

Set B

bats   Nat   man

bin   bib   cabs

READ THE SENTENCES

Set C

1. She can bat.

2. I sat with an ant.

3. She can pat it.

4. Nat sat with me.

5. He can sip it.

© Pearson Education

Note to Teacher Set A: Children read each word. Set B: Children read each word.
Set C: Children read one or two sentences.

Little Panda

COMPARE AND CONTRAST

Color the things that are alike. Draw an *X* on things that are different.

Anna Panda

Anna Panda

Note to Teacher Have children compare and contrast the two pictures. Have them color things that are the same. Have them draw an *X* over things that are different.

© Pearson Education

READ THE WORDS

Set A

rat   ram

rib   ran

READ MORE WORDS

Set B

rip   rats   rap

rim   bat   ribs

READ THE SENTENCES

Set C

1. I bit the pit.

2. The rat can sit.

3. She ran with me.

4. My cat likes to nap.

5. We have a mat for me.

Note to Teacher Set A: Children read each word. Set B: Children read each word.
Set C: Children read one or two sentences.

Little Quack

© Pearson Education

PLOT

Put these pictures in order to show
the plot of "The Ugly Duckling."

Note to Teacher Have children cut out the boxes and glue them on another sheet of paper in the correct order of the story.

© Pearson Education

READ THE WORDS

Set A

kid	did
Kim	dip

READ MORE WORDS

Set B

kit	kiss	dab
sad	kin	Dan

READ THE SENTENCES

Set C

1. The cat can see the rat.

2. Little Dan can look in the pan.

3. We like my little cat, Kim.

4. I have a mat.

5. Kim naps with me.

Note to Teacher Set A: Children read each word. Set B: Children read each word.
Set C: Children read one or two sentences.

See How We Grow

© Pearson Education

CAUSE AND EFFECT

Cut out the pictures. Glue them in the right box.

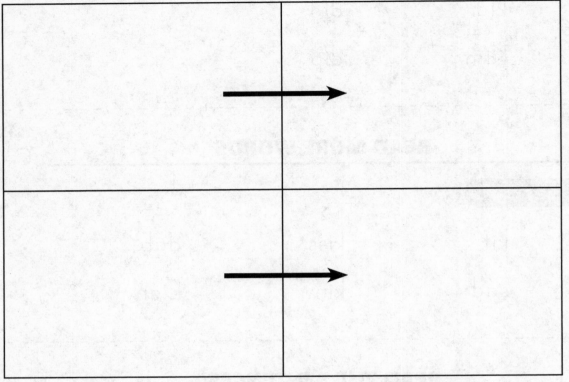

Note to Teacher Have children cut out pictures and glue them in the correct box.

© Pearson Education

READ THE WORDS

Set A

fan   fit

kid   if

 -

READ MORE WORDS

Set B

fin   fad   fib

fits   fat   fans

 -

READ THE SENTENCES

Set C

1. I see a kit.

2. Look for the little cat.

3. She ran with me.

4. The fin is little.

5. We like to look at the bat.

Note to Teacher Set A: Children read each word. Set B: Children read each word. Set C: Children read one or two sentences.

Farfallina and Marcel

© Pearson Education

PLOT

Put these events from "Otis" in order.

Note to Teacher Have children cut out the scenes and glue them in the correct order on a separate sheet of paper.

© Pearson Education

READ THE WORDS

Set A

top   cot

on   fog

READ MORE WORDS

Set B

dot   mop   Rob

mom   pop   sod

READ THE SENTENCES

Set C

1. Ron sat on the mat with you.

2. The mop is on the cot.

3. They have a lot of pots.

4. Look at the cat on top.

5. We got a trip to the pond.

Note to Teacher Set A: Children read each word. Set B: Children read each word.
Set C: Children read one or two sentences.

Seeds

© Pearson Education

DRAW CONCLUSIONS

Add to the picture the things that will help the seeds grow.

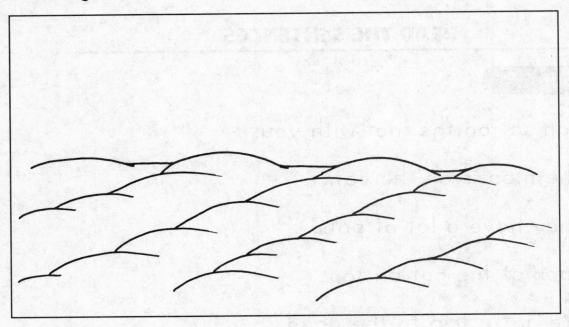

Draw what will happen to the seeds.

Note to Teacher Have children complete the first picture, adding the things they think seeds need to grow. Then have them draw what will happen to the seeds.

© Pearson Education

READ THE WORDS

Set A

dot   Ron   pop   rod

READ MORE WORDS

Set B

not   pots   pods

nod   Tom   dots

READ THE SENTENCES

Set C

1. Tom sees the map.

2. They like my little cat.

3. The dog stops to hop.

4. You have the pots.

5. He sat on top of the bin.

Note to Teacher Set A: Children read each word. Set B: Children read each word.
Set C: Children read one or two sentences.

Hide, Clyde!

© Pearson Education

MAIN IDEA

Color the picture that shows the main idea of "Color Me Chameleon."

Note to Teacher Have children identify and color the picture that shows the main idea.

© Pearson Education

© Pearson Education

Name _____ Date _____

Day 5 Assessment Chart

Unit 3

	Record Assessment Data and Calculate Score		Reteach ✓	Reassess
	Total Possible	Child's Number Correct		
Week 1 *Little Panda*				
A Read the Words	4			
B Read More Words	6			
C Read the Sentences	5			
Week 2 *Little Quack*				
A Read the Words	4			
B Read More Words	6			
C Read the Sentences	5			
Week 3 *See How We Grow*				
A Read the Words	4			
B Read More Words	6			
C Read the Sentences	5			
Week 4 *Farfallina and Marcel*				
A Read the Words	4			
B Read More Words	6			
C Read the Sentences	5			
Week 5 *Seeds*				
A Read the Words	4			
B Read More Words	6			
C Read the Sentences	5			
Week 6 *Hide, Clyde!*				
A Read the Words	4			
B Read More Words	6			
C Read the Sentences	5			
	90			

- **RECORD SCORES** In the Child's Number Correct column, record scores for the set(s) of the Day 5 Assessment used.
- **RETEACH SKILLS** If a child is unable to successfully complete Sets A and/or B, then reteach the skills using the Reteach lessons on pp. DI·45–DI·50.

- **REASSESS** Use the same set of assessments or an easier set for reassessment.

READ THE WORDS

Set A

hip   hop

hot   had

READ MORE WORDS

Set B

hat   ham   hid

Hap   hot   him

READ THE SENTENCES

Set C

1. Hap can stop for it.

2. Are you at the spot?

3. That is Hob.

4. The pot had that top.

5. The pan is not hot.

Note to Teacher Set A: Children read each word. Set B: Children read each word.
Set C: Children read one or two sentences.

Bunny Day

© Pearson Education

SEQUENCE

Put these events from "A Day Like Every Other Day" in order.

Note to Teacher Have children cut out the scenes and glue them in the correct order onto another piece of paper.

© Pearson Education

READ THE WORDS

Set A

lip	lap
lad	lid

READ MORE WORDS

Set B

fill	lob	mill
hill	doll	Bill

READ THE SENTENCES

Set C

1. Dan is a sad lad.

2. That is my cap.

3. You are a little cat.

4. Did Bill and Lil go to see the pit?

5. Do Dan and Bill have dill?

Note to Teacher Set A: Children read each word. Set B: Children read each word.
Set C: Children read one or two sentences.

My Lucky Day

© Pearson Education

CAUSE AND EFFECT

Color the top picture. Color the one picture at the bottom that makes it happen.

Note to Teacher Have children color the large scene and the one other picture that makes the large scene happen.

© Pearson Education

READ THE WORDS

Set A

spot   flat

crib   trap

READ MORE WORDS

Set B

hand   spin   clap

mask   trip   mist

READ THE SENTENCES

Set C

1. I have one fast raft.

2. We can see three drops.

3. Two kids are with me.

4. Look at the four maps.

5. Five masks are a lot.

Note to Teacher Set A: Children read each word. Set B: Children read each word.
Set C: Children read one or two sentences.

One Little Mouse

© Pearson Education

Put events from "The Tale of Peter Rabbit" in order.

Note to Teacher Have children cut out the scenes from the story and glue them onto another paper in sequential order. Have them label the sequence 1–3.

© Pearson Education

READ THE WORDS

Set A

got   dig

gas   log

✂- ✂

READ MORE WORDS

Set B

dog   glad   grab

grin   pig   flag

✂- ✂

READ THE SENTENCES

Set C

1. I see a grin on the pig.

2. The big dog can dig.

3. The dog is with me.

4. I got a little flag.

5. Can you tag me?

Note to Teacher Set A: Children read each word. Set B: Children read each word.
Set C: Children read one or two sentences.

Goldilocks and the Three Bears

© Pearson Education

CHARACTER

Draw the characters from "A Canary's Song."

Huey

The Canary

Note to Teacher Have children draw the two characters from "A Canary's Song" in the appropriate boxes.

© Pearson Education

READ THE WORDS

Set A

hen   pen   left   egg

✂ - ✂

READ MORE WORDS

Set B

pet   dress   lend

beg   sent   mend

✂ - ✂

READ THE SENTENCES

Set C

1. Ben is here in the den.

2. The red net is on top of the well.

3. Len and Ken go to the pen.

4. Meg is my little hen.

5. The men went to get a pet.

Note to Teacher Set A: Children read each word. Set B: Children read each word.
Set C: Children read one or two sentences.

If You Could Go to Antarctica

© Pearson Education

CLASSIFY AND CATEGORIZE

Cut out the pictures and glue them on the correct side of the chart.

At Snow Hill	At the Ocean

Note to Teacher Have children cut out pictures and glue them on the appropriate side of the T-chart.

© Pearson Education

READ THE WORDS

Set A

Ted   leg   send

sled

  -

READ MORE WORDS

Set B

bell   melt   send

spend   help   step

- -

READ THE SENTENCES

Set C

1. I can ring my bell from here.

2. I have a little red hen.

3. Ned will come to see me.

4. My pet can look here.

5. Tell Ted to go with you.

Note to Teacher Set A: Children read each word. Set B: Children read each word.
Set C: Children read one or two sentences.

Abuela

© Pearson Education

SETTING

Draw where each part of the story happens.

Polly and her parents wait for Gran at the airport.

Gran and Polly take a walk.

Gran and Polly have a tea party.

Note to Teacher Have children fill in the setting in each picture by drawing the background for each of the three scenes.

© Pearson Education

Day 5 Assessment Chart — Unit 4

	Record Assessment Data and Calculate Score		Reteach ✓	Reassess
	Total Possible	Child's Number Correct		
Week 1 *Bunny Day*				
A Read the Words	4			
B Read More Words	6			
C Read the Sentences	5			
Week 2 *My Lucky Day*				
A Read the Words	4			
B Read More Words	6			
C Read the Sentences	5			
Week 3 *One Little Mouse*				
A Read the Words	4			
B Read More Words	6			
C Read the Sentences	5			
Week 4 *Goldilocks and the Three Bears*				
A Read the Words	4			
B Read More Words	6			
C Read the Sentences	5			
Week 5 *If You Could Go to Antarctica*				
A Read the Words	4			
B Read More Words	6			
C Read the Sentences	5			
Week 6 *Abuela*				
A Read the Words	4			
B Read More Words	6			
C Read the Sentences	5			
	90			

- **RECORD SCORES** In the Child's Number Correct column, record scores for the set(s) of the Day 5 Assessment used.
- **RETEACH SKILLS** If a child is unable to successfully complete Sets A and/or B, then reteach the skills using the Reteach lessons on pp. DI·45–DI·50.

- **REASSESS** Use the same set of assessments or an easier set for reassessment.

© Pearson Education

READ THE WORDS

Set A

Wes   jet

win   Jan

✂ - ✂

READ MORE WORDS

Set B

will   jets   web

went   Jill   jig

✂ - ✂

READ THE SENTENCES

Set C

1. Wes sat in the little blue jet.

2. Jem will win the hat.

3. Jan had a big yellow bag.

4. The blue jet is fast.

5. Will Jan win the green hat?

Note to Teacher Set A: Children read each word. Set B: Children read each word.
Set C: Children read one or two sentences.

Max Takes the Train

© Pearson Education

REALISM AND FANTASY

Color the make-believe picture.

Note to Teacher Have children color the scene that is make-believe.

© Pearson Education

READ THE WORDS

Set A

fox	fix
wax	Rex

READ MORE WORDS

Set B

next	box	tax
mix	Max	six

READ THE SENTENCES

Set C

1. I like to mix mud.

2. Jan can wax the yellow box.

3. They like to go on a jet.

4. Rex and I look in the little green cup.

5. Will the blue hat fit?

Note to Teacher Set A: Children read each word. Set B: Children read each word.
Set C: Children read one or two sentences.

Mayday! Mayday!

© Pearson Education

CAUSE AND EFFECT

Color the picture that shows what happened in "The Mysteries of Flight." Then color the picture that shows why it happened.

What happened?

Why did it happen?

Note to Teacher Have children color the large picture of what happened in the story. Then have them choose and color the picture showing why it happened.

© Pearson Education

READ THE WORDS

Set A

cup   up

rug   tub

READ MORE WORDS

Set B

bump   drum   dust

jump   club   plum

READ THE SENTENCES

Set C

1. Bud gets a hug from Mom.

2. What was in the box?

3. They said, "Bud is in the tub."

4. She said, "Mud is fun."

5. You said the bug was big.

Note to Teacher Set A: Children read each word. Set B: Children read each word.
Set C: Children read one or two sentences.

Messenger, Messenger

© Pearson Education

COMPARE AND CONTRAST

Color the things that are alike in the two pictures. Cross out the things that are different.

Note to Teacher Have children practice comparing and contrasting by coloring things that are the same and crossing out things that are different in the two pictures.

© Pearson Education

READ THE WORDS

Set A

mug   nut

cub   bug

- -

READ MORE WORDS

Set B

jump   suds   drum

club   stun   dust

- -

READ THE SENTENCES

Set C

1. What is in the cup?

2. He dug in the mud.

3. Was a bug on the rug?

4. Is the pup a gift for me?

5. Dad said, "I can see a little bit left."

Note to Teacher Set A: Children read each word. Set B: Children read each word.
Set C: Children read one or two sentences.

The Little Engine That Could

© Pearson Education

PLOT

Color the boy in his bed. Then color the picture that shows what he finds out.

Note to Teacher Have children color the picture of the boy and what he discovers.

© Pearson Education

READ THE WORDS

Set A

zip   jazz

van   Bev

- -

READ MORE WORDS

Set B

buzz   zap   vest

frizz   Val   vet

- -

READ THE SENTENCES

Set C

1. Dad likes the jazz band.

2. Come with me.

3. Where is the map?

4. Will you come with me?

5. Val rode in the big bus.

© Pearson Education

Note to Teacher Set A: Children read each word. Set B: Children read each word. Set C: Children read one or two sentences.

On the Move!

MAIN IDEA

Color the picture that shows the main idea.

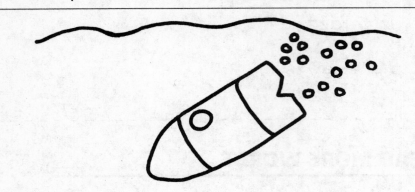

Note to Teacher Have children color the picture that shows the correct main idea.

© Pearson Education

READ THE WORDS

Set A

quit   yell

quiz   yak

✂ - ✂

READ MORE WORDS

Set B

quilt   yam   yaks

Quinn   quill   yes

✂ - ✂

READ THE SENTENCES

Set C

1. Jim will like the little quiz.

2. Dad will not quit.

3. Where are Mom and Dad?

4. Come quick! The ox ran up a hill.

5. The yellow yak can jump.

© Pearson Education

Note to Teacher Set A: Children read each word. Set B: Children read each word.
Set C: Children read one or two sentences.

This Is the Way We Go to School

DRAW CONCLUSIONS

Draw conclusions about what might happen next.

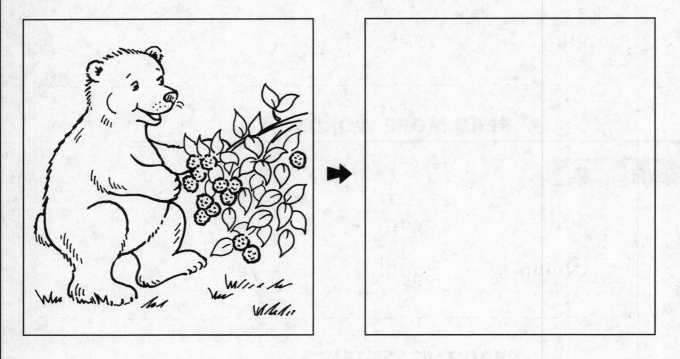

Note to Teacher Review the illustrations with children. Have the children decide and draw what might happen next.

© Pearson Education

Day 5 Assessment Chart Unit 5

	Record Assessment Data and Calculate Score		Reteach ✓	Reassess
	Total Possible	Child's Number Correct		
Week 1 *Max Takes the Train*				
A Read the Words	4			
B Read More Words	6			
C Read the Sentences	5			
Week 2 *Mayday! Mayday!*				
A Read the Words	4			
B Read More Words	6			
C Read the Sentences	5			
Week 3 *Messenger, Messenger*				
A Read the Words	4			
B Read More Words	6			
C Read the Sentences	5			
Week 4 *The Little Engine That Could*				
A Read the Words	4			
B Read More Words	6			
C Read the Sentences	5			
Week 5 *On the Move!*				
A Read the Words	4			
B Read More Words	6			
C Read the Sentences	5			
Week 6 *This Is the Way We Go to School*				
A Read the Words	4			
B Read More Words	6			
C Read the Sentences	5			
	90			

- **RECORD SCORES** In the Child's Number Correct column, record scores for the set(s) of the Day 5 Assessment used.
- **RETEACH SKILLS** If a child is unable to successfully complete Sets A and/or B, then reteach the skills using the Reteach lessons on pp. DI·45–DI·50.

- **REASSESS** Use the same set of assessments or an easier set for reassessment.

© Pearson Education

READ THE WORDS

Set A

pat	hid	rip
lap	wig	sad

READ MORE WORDS

Set B

spin	man	quit
tip	snap	sit
yak	camp	bat

READ THE SENTENCES

Set C

1. Jan hid the pig.

2. She pets the cats.

3. Ned had a big van.

4. Jill can sit on the lid.

5. I am glad you are not sad.

Note to Teacher Set A: Children read each word. Set B: Children read each word.
Set C: Children read one or two sentences.

Homes Around the World

© Pearson Education

COMPARE AND CONTRAST

Sort these pictures. Which belong with "House of Snow"? Which belong with a city house?

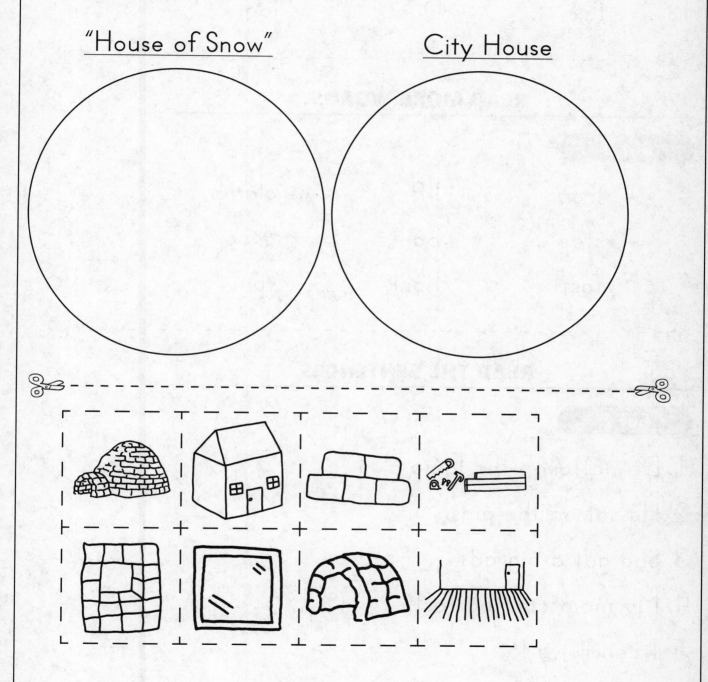

"House of Snow"   City House

Note to Teacher Have children color the pictures. Then cut out the pictures and glue them in the correct circle.

READ THE WORDS

Set A

lot	hot	yam
fox	Dan	jog

READ MORE WORDS

Set B

frog	lift	clamp
stop	pants	drop
fast	honk	spin

READ THE SENTENCES

Set C

1. Do not drop the lamp.

2. He sat on the pins.

3. She got a big gift.

4. My mom can jog fast.

5. I can lift a lot.

Note to Teacher Set A: Children read each word. Set B: Children read each word. *Old MacDonald had a Woodshop*
Set C: Children read one or two sentences.

© Pearson Education

Color the characters from "The Elves and the Shoemaker."

Note to Teacher Have children color the characters from "The Elves and the Shoemaker."

© Pearson Education

READ THE WORDS

Set A

pet	nest	hen
jog	win	pad

✂ - ✂

READ MORE WORDS

Set B

bend	step	crib
last	drip	next
kept	jump	rest

✂ - ✂

READ THE SENTENCES

Set C

1. I can fix the bell.

2. Ted had a pet hen.

3. We step in the mud.

4. We can not jump on the bed.

5. They jog to the big pond.

Note to Teacher Set A: Children read each word. Set B: Children read each word. Set C: Children read one or two sentences.

Building Beavers

© Pearson Education

222

MAIN IDEA

Color the picture that shows what "Robin's Nest" is all about.

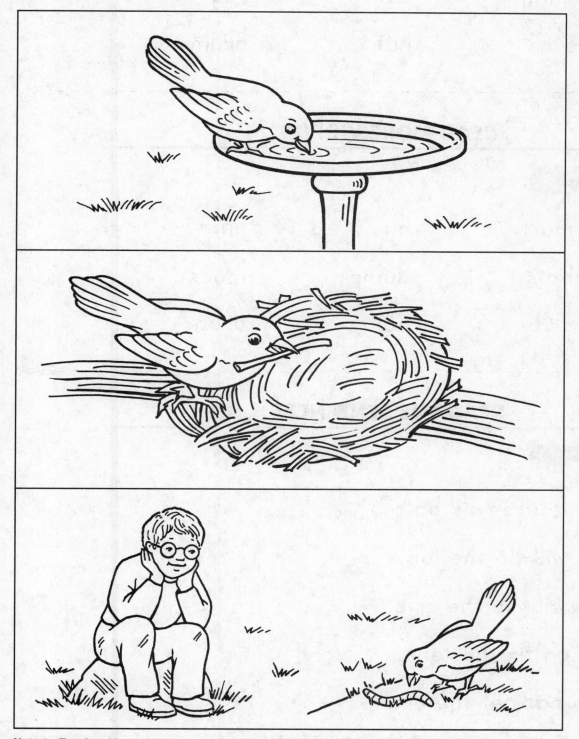

Note to Teacher Have children color the picture that shows the main idea of the story.

© Pearson Education

READ THE WORDS

Set A

bump	cut	rug
sun	hut	drum

READ MORE WORDS

Set B

must	hits	hunt
bats	dump	mugs
club	bun	drop

READ THE SENTENCES

Set C

1. Can you see six bats?

2. They will do the job.

3. She is not in the crib.

4. We can fix the tent.

5. I can not get the drum.

Note to Teacher Set A: Children read each word. Set B: Children read each word.
Set C: Children read one or two sentences.

The Night Worker

© Pearson Education

PLOT

Show the beginning, middle, and end of "Night in the Country."

Note to Teacher Have children cut out the boxes and glue them on another sheet of paper in the correct story order.

© Pearson Education

READ THE WORDS

Set A

bug	zip	jug
log	ant	end

✂ - ✂

READ MORE WORDS

Set B

went	spot	bump
trip	frog	crabs
list	hugs	club

✂ - ✂

READ THE SENTENCES

Set C

1. My hat is in the box.

2. The dogs jump on the bed.

3. Will you pet the pig?

4. Send the gift to Pam.

5. She went on a trip.

Note to Teacher Set A: Children read each word. Set B: Children read each word. Set C: Children read one or two sentences.

The House That Tony Lives In

© Pearson Education

SETTING

Color the picture that shows "A House
by the Sea."

Note to Teacher Have children color the picture that is an appropriate setting for the story.

© Pearson Education

READ THE WORDS

Set A

wax	jog	nut
six	met	bug

 -

READ MORE WORDS

Set B

pens	glad	vest
cast	digs	frog
huts	mask	drop

READ THE SENTENCES

Set C

1. Did you see the frog?

2. Can I have the gift?

3. She has the best tent in the land.

4. The duck and the pig got on the bus.

5. The egg is in the pan.

Note to Teacher Set A: Children read each word. Set B: Children read each word.
Set C: Children read one or two sentences.

Animal Homes

© Pearson Education

DRAW CONCLUSIONS

Color the house for the animal.

Note to Teacher Have children use the information in the text and what they already know to color the house for each animal.

© Pearson Education

229

Day 5 Assessment Chart

Unit 6

	Record Assessment Data and Calculate Score		Reteach ✓	Reassess
	Total Possible	Child's Number Correct		
Week 1 *Homes Around the World*				
A Read the Words	6			
B Read More Words	9			
C Read the Sentences	5			
Week 2 *Old MacDonald had a Woodshop*				
A Read the Words	6			
B Read More Words	9			
C Read the Sentences	5			
Week 3 *Building Beavers*				
A Read the Words	6			
B Read More Words	9			
C Read the Sentences	5			
Week 4 *The Night Worker*				
A Read the Words	6			
B Read More Words	9			
C Read the Sentences	5			
Week 5 *The House That Tony Lives In*				
A Read the Words	6			
B Read More Words	9			
C Read the Sentences	5			
Week 6 *Animal Homes*				
A Read the Words	6			
B Read More Words	9			
C Read the Sentences	5			
	120			

- **RECORD SCORES** In the Child's Number Correct column, record scores for the set(s) of the Day 5 Assessment used.
- **RETEACH SKILLS** If a child is unable to successfully complete Sets A and/or B, then reteach the skills using the Reteach lessons on pp. DI·45–DI·50.
- **REASSESS** Use the same set of assessments or an easier set for reassessment.

© Pearson Education

Monitoring Progress Forms for Grade 1

From *Scott Foresman Reading Street* Teacher's Editions

© Pearson Education

Fluency Progress Chart, Grade 1

Name

	1	2	3	4	5	6	7	8	9	10	11	12	13	14	15	16	17	18	19	20	21	22	23	24	25	26	27	28	29	30
110																														
105																														
100																														
95																														
90																														
85																														
80																														
75																														
70																														
65																														
60																														
55																														
50																														
45																														
40																														
35																														
30																														
25																														
20																														
15																														

Timed Reading

© Pearson Education

READ THE WORDS

Name _____

Mark correct response.   Mark correct response.

cat ▢   at ▢

in ▢   sack ▢

tap ▢   on ▢

back ▢   pack ▢

way ▢   hat ▢

man ▢   tack ▢

Scoring: Score 1 point for each correct answer.

Short *a (cat, tap, man, at, hat)* _____ / __5__

Final *ck (back, sack, pack, tack)* _____ / __4__

High-Frequency Words *(in, way, on)* _____ / __3__

© Pearson Education

READ THE SENTENCES

Set A

1. Pam is on the way back.
2. The hat is on the rack.
3. Mack is in the cab.
4. Jack ran that way.
5. The cat is on the pack.
6. The ham is in the sack.

Set B

1. We go back that way for gas.
2. Look at the yellow hat on the rack.
3. Dad has a blue cap in the sack.
4. Jack sat in the green van.
5. The little tack is on the mat.
6. That is the way I pack a bag.

Set C

1. Jack drove the van all the way home.
2. Push in the tack so the map stays up.
3. Max put all the books back on the shelf.
4. Does Zack know the way to Pat's house?
5. Mack put jam on wheat bread.
6. She said to go in and hang your hat on the rack.

© Pearson Education

READ THE WORDS

Name _____

Mark correct response.　　　　　　Mark correct response.

on　　　☐　　　six　　　☐

mix　　　☐　　　up　　　☐

fix　　　☐　　　Max　　　☐

and　　　☐　　　sit　　　☐

it　　　☐　　　did　　　☐

in　　　☐　　　way　　　☐

take　　　☐　　　wig　　　☐

Scoring: Score 1 point for each correct answer.
Short *i (it, in, sit, did, wig)* _____ / _5_
Final *x (mix, fix, six, Max)* _____ / _4_
High-Frequency Words *(on, and, take, up, way)* _____ / _5_

© Pearson Education

READ THE SENTENCES

Set A

1. Tim can take the mix.
2. Mix it up!
3. Take the mix, Jim.
4. Jim can mix it up.
5. Mix it and fix it!
6. Max can lick it up!

Set B

1. Tim and Sam can mix it up.
2. Take the mix and fix it, Kim!
3. Kim and Sam can fix it up!
4. Tim, come back and see me at six.
5. Take the mix and fix it quick!
6. Tim the Cat can lick and mix!

Set C

1. Jim and Jan take three big licks of that mix.
2. Will three licks fill Jim up until six?
3. Jim will take more and more licks of mix!
4. Pam and Sam will take more mix.
5. Did Tim and Kim each get six licks?
6. Tim licked up six spoonfuls of tasty mix!

© Pearson Education

READ THE WORDS

Name _____

Mark correct response.   Mark correct response.

get   ☐   hats   ☐

pop   ☐   wigs   ☐

hot   ☐   packs   ☐

mom   ☐   fox   ☐

pots   ☐   help   ☐

rocks   ☐   use   ☐

Scoring: Score 1 point for each correct answer.

Short o (pop, hot, mom, fox) _____ / __4__

-s Plurals (pots, rocks, hats, wigs, packs) _____ / __5__

High-Frequency Words (get, help, use) _____ / __3__

© Pearson Education

READ THE SENTENCES

Set A

1. Pop can help pack the pots.
2. Mom can get the hats.
3. Help me pack the wigs.
4. Get six pots to pack in the box.
5. Use a pot to get rocks.
6. Use hats to fan hot cats.

Set B

1. Mom and I use hot pots.
2. Help Pop pack the wigs.
3. Use a box to pack the hats.
4. Help Pop hop on the rocks.
5. Use the fans to fix hot cats.
6. Mom can help me get the cats.

Set C

1. Get the rocks that are not wet.
2. Pop can help fix those rocks.
3. Pop can use big pots of sand.
4. Use hats to help if you get hot.
5. Help Mom pack a box of wigs.
6. Two cats get a box of hats.

© Pearson Education

READ THE WORDS

Name _____

Mark correct response.   Mark correct response.

hops	☐	licks	☐
packs	☐	packing	☐
taps	☐	picking	☐
eat	☐	rocking	☐
her	☐	sits	☐
kicking	☐	this	☐
naps	☐	too	☐

Scoring: Score 1 point for each correct answer.

Inflected Ending -s *(hops, packs, taps, naps, licks, sits)* _____ /__6__

Inflected Ending -ing *(kicking, packing, picking, rocking)* _____ /__4__

High-Frequency Words *(eat, her, this, too)* _____ /__4__

© Pearson Education

READ THE SENTENCES

Set A

1. Tim helps by picking up this bag.
2. Jack sits packing mix to eat.
3. He sits licking mix too.
4. The cat sits rocking in her box.
5. The cat sits here licking too.
6. This little box sits here ticking.

Set B

1. The fox is picking up her kit that naps.
2. The kit sits licking up her mix.
3. Dad looks at the cat licking her mat.
4. This cat eats by licking the can.
5. Tim helps this cat that is kicking.
6. Mom sits rocking this cat that naps.

Set C

1. This cat plays a kicking game with her ball.
2. Jan helps by packing the hats in her big box.
3. Dad helps the team win by kicking a goal too.
4. Mom laughs as she packs up her little blue sack.
5. Mom sits here packing a box of things to eat.
6. Pam picks some fruit from the tree growing in her yard.

© Pearson Education

READ THE WORDS

Name _____

Mark correct response.　　　　　　　Mark correct response.

bed　　☐　┊　saw　　☐

Ben　　☐　┊　sled　　☐

Fred　　☐　┊　small　　☐

frog　　☐　┊　spot　　☐

traps　☐　┊　tree　　☐

net　　☐　┊　wet　　☐

fed　　☐　┊　your　　☐

Scoring: Score 1 point for each correct answer.

Short *e (bed, Ben, net, fed, wet)* _____ /__5__

Initial Blends *(Fred, frog, traps, sled, spot)* _____ /__5__

High-Frequency Words *(saw, small, tree, your)* _____ /__4__

© Pearson Education

READ THE SENTENCES

Set A

1. Pop saw a wet frog.
2. Fred, get your net.
3. The small frog is wet.
4. Ben, get your sled.
5. Fran naps in your tree.
6. A frog naps on your bed.

Set B

1. Jen can take your sled.
2. Ben saw a green spot there.
3. We met Fred at the tree.
4. Brett likes your sled too.
5. Ben, come see your frog.
6. The small frog naps on a wet rock.

Set C

1. Ben saw a frog flop into the lake.
2. Fred watched a hen peck at a tree.
3. Jack met Fred under the big tree.
4. Your cat finds a spot on the bed and naps.
5. Bring your sled to the spot on the hill.
6. Get your wet frog out of the net.

© Pearson Education

READ THE WORDS

Name _____

Mark correct response.   Mark correct response.

home	☐	pups	☐
bus	☐	pond	☐
must	☐	hugs	☐
sun	☐	stump	☐
into	☐	mud	☐
rest	☐	them	☐
jump	☐	slug	☐
many	☐	just	☐

Scoring: Score 1 point for each correct answer.

Short *u (bus, pups, hugs, mud, sun, slug)* _____ /__6__

Final Blends *(must, rest, jump, pond, stump, just)* _____ /__6__

High-Frequency Words *(home, into, many, them)* _____ /__4__

© Pearson Education

READ THE SENTENCES

Set A

1. Gus must take mud home for his frogs.
2. Gus puts them into a pond.
3. Go home and hug your pups.
4. You can jump into bed, Gus.
5. Russ can rest on his bed at home.
6. He must get many hugs from Mom.

Set B

1. Gus runs and jumps into the pond.
2. Many small frogs swim in the big pond.
3. Frogs and pups jump into the pond.
4. Mom dug into the mud to get a plant.
5. Russ watched them swim from a stump.
6. Mom said that you must come home to rest, Gus.

Set C

1. Gus hugged his pups and then watched them jump.
2. Pug saw many frogs jump in the mud.
3. Mom chased her pups into the pond.
4. Sunny sat on a stump until she went home.
5. Punky saw her pups crawl home to rest.
6. Rusty just ran home with the milk in his hand.

© Pearson Education

Sentence Reading Chart

Unit 1

	Phonics		High-Frequency		Reteach ✓	Reassess: Words Correct
	Total Words	Words Correct	Total Words	Words Correct		
Week 1 *Sam, Come Back!* A B C						
Short *a*	7					
Final *ck*	6					
High-Frequency Words			5			
Week 2 *Pig in a Wig* A B C						
Short *i*	8					
Final *x*	7					
High-Frequency Words			7			
Week 3 *The Big Blue Ox* A B C						
Short *o*	6					
-s Plurals	7					
High-Frequency Words			5			
Week 4 *A Fox and a Kit* A B C						
Inflected Ending -s	8					
Inflected Ending -ing	6					
High-Frequency Words			6			
Week 5 *Get the Egg!* A B C						
Short *e*	7					
Initial Blends	7					
High-Frequency Words			6			
Week 6 *Animal Park* A B C						
Short *u*	8					
Final Blends	8					
High-Frequency Words			6			
Unit Scores	**85**		**29**			

- **RECORD SCORES** Use this chart to record scores for the Day 5 Sentence Reading Assessment. Circle A, B, or C to record which set of sentences was used.

- **RETEACH PHONICS SKILLS** If the child is unable to read all the tested phonics words, then reteach the phonics skills using the Reteach lessons on pp. DI·76–DI·84.

- **PRACTICE HIGH-FREQUENCY WORDS** If the child is unable to read all the tested high-frequency words, then provide additional practice for the week's words. See pp. 28e, 50e, 72e, 92e, 112e, and 132e.

- **REASSESS** Use the same set of sentences or an easier set for reassessment.

© Pearson Education

READ THE WORDS

Name _____

Mark correct response.   Mark correct response.

good   ☐   this   ☐

dash   ☐   catch   ☐

shop   ☐   bath   ☐

no   ☐   walk   ☐

wall   ☐   put   ☐

path   ☐   fall   ☐

small   ☐   wish   ☐

want   ☐   talk   ☐

Scoring: Score 1 point for each correct answer.

Digraphs *sh, th (dash, shop, path, this, bath, wish)* _____ /__6__

Sound of *a* in *ball (wall, small, walk, fall, talk)* _____ /__5__

High-Frequency Words *(good, no, want, catch, put)* _____ /__5__

© Pearson Education

READ THE SENTENCES

Set A

1. That was a good walk.
2. A small slug has no shell.
3. Dan put the salts in the bath.
4. Pam shall catch the ball.
5. Sam wants all the fish.
6. Jan can put it on the tall shelf.

Set B

1. Max went on a good walk with Ted.
2. We saw no small shells in the sand.
3. Do not put the fish in the bath.
4. Can she catch the ball with her mitt?
5. All the fish in the pond want to swim.
6. We put all the big bins up on the shelf.

Set C

1. Our dog went for a good walk with Mom and Dad.
2. Ann had no small shells in her bag when she got home.
3. Todd ran water in the bathtub and then put his ship in it.
4. Jan felt sad that she did not catch the ball in her mitt.
5. Jim and Bob want to trap all the fish in the pond.
6. We could not put the tall books on the shelf.

© Pearson Education

READ THE WORDS

Name _____

Mark correct response.   Mark correct response.

late ☐   stage ☐

name ☐   cent ☐

could ☐   horse ☐

page ☐   game ☐

face ☐   gate ☐

paper ☐   rake ☐

rage ☐   old ☐

be ☐   trace ☐

lace ☐   shape ☐

Scoring: Score 1 point for each correct answer.
Long *a* Words (*late, name, game, gate, rake, shape*) _____ / _6_
c/s/, *g*/j/ Words (*page, face, rage, lace, stage, cent, trace*) _____ / _7_
High-Frequency Words (*could, paper, be, horse, old*) _____ / _5_

© Pearson Education

READ THE SENTENCES

Set A

1. The tame horse can race.
2. Don made a face on paper.
3. A game will be on stage.
4. We had an old cage for sale.
5. Place the plate on the paper.
6. Dan could make fudge.

Set B

1. We saw the same horse win a race.
2. Don made a pig face on a paper bag.
3. It will be too late to go on stage.
4. Beth got an old dog cage at the sale.
5. We put the plate on a paper place mat.
6. Dan could make some fudge to sell.

Set C

1. The horse with the tan mane won the race.
2. Don made a paper bag mask with a pig face.
3. We will be too late to see the band on stage.
4. Beth had a sale to sell her old dog cage.
5. The plate looks good on the paper place mat.
6. Dan could sell all the fudge that Jan can make.

© Pearson Education

READ THE WORDS

Name _____

Mark correct response.   Mark correct response.

people ☐   smile ☐

chip ☐   patch ☐

work ☐   out ☐

which ☐   pine ☐

nine ☐   when ☐

hatch ☐   lunch ☐

live ☐   match ☐

nice ☐   bite ☐

who ☐   chick ☐

while ☐   pile ☐

Scoring: Score 1 point for each correct answer.

Long *i* (*nine, nice, smile, pine, bite, pile*) _____ / __6__

Digraphs *wh, ch, tch* (*chip, which, hatch,*
   while, patch, when, lunch, match, chick) _____ / __9__

High-Frequency Words (*people, work, live, who, out*) _____ / __5__

© Pearson Education

READ THE SENTENCES

Set A

1. People like to play catch.
2. When will it be time to go out?
3. Who can patch my kite?
4. Tim works at lunch all the time.
5. They live on a fine ranch.
6. A cat went out to catch the mice.

Set B

1. People like to play catch with a ball.
2. When will it be time for us to go out?
3. Is Dad the one who can patch my kite?
4. Mitch went out to play with his ship.
5. The horses live on a fine ranch.
6. My cat looks out for mice to catch.

Set C

1. Many people like to toss and catch a ball.
2. Will you tell us when it is time to go out?
3. Who can patch my kite with paper and tape?
4. Tom eats lunch at work all the time.
5. We went to live on a fine ranch for a month.
6. My cat will sit and watch for mice to come out.

© Pearson Education

READ THE SENTENCES

Set A

1. Ants can't fall down a hole.
2. I'm inside my home.
3. We'll ride home together.
4. There isn't a note for Jim.
5. Now I'm sad I broke my bike.
6. He'll dig down for a bone.

Set B

1. Ants can't lift a cake down a hole.
2. I'm not sad inside my home.
3. We'll all ride back home together.
4. There isn't a note in this box.
5. Now I'm glad that I rode my bike.
6. He'll dig deep down for a bone.

Set C

1. Many ants can't take a cake down a hole.
2. I can play when I'm inside my home.
3. We'll all ride home on the bus together.
4. There isn't a note in this box for me.
5. Now I'm glad that I rode my bike up the hill.
6. When the dog is here, he'll dig down for a bone.

© Pearson Education

Joe's T-Rex

"I'll dig for bones," said Joe.   6
"I hope to get a T-Rex."   12

He dug. He hit a bump.   18
"I hope it is a bone," said Joe.   26
"I'll get down and look."   31

"It is just a stone," said Joe.   38
"I'll dig more."   41

He dug.   43
The stone didn't budge.   47

Joe got a rope. He put it on the stone.   57
He gave the rope a tug.   63
The stone didn't budge.   67

"This stone won't go," said Joe.   73
"I can't get a T-Rex like this."   80

Rose came and said, "Did you get a T-Rex?"   89

"No T-Rex!" said Joe.   93
"I dug for a stone. There it is!"   101

© Pearson Education

READ THE SENTENCES

Set A

1. A huge bear hunted for food.
2. Steve camped where pines grow.
3. We wanted to find a cute pup.
4. Pete walked all around here.
5. The mule kicked the water dish.
6. He crushed a tube under a box.

Set B

1. A huge bear cub hunted for its food.
2. Steve camped in a tent where pines grow.
3. We wanted to find a cute pup to take home.
4. Pete walked around here for a long time.
5. The mule spilled the water in his dish.
6. He crushed a cube of ice under a box.

Set C

1. A huge bear hunted for food in the forest.
2. Steve camped in an old tent where pines grow.
3. We wanted to find a cute pup for our new pet.
4. Pete walked here and there and all around.
5. The mule kicked the water dish out the gate.
6. He crushed a bunch of ice cubes under a huge box.

© Pearson Education

The Log

June walked with Dan.	4
They saw a log.	8
Dan wanted to sit on the log.	15
"Ants! Ants are on this log!" said Dan.	23
"The log is their home," said June.	30
"It is their food.	34
Ants dig inside.	37
They make a nest inside.	42
They can eat the log."	47
"Look around the end," said Dan.	53
"The log is like a tube."	59
"The log is soft," said June.	65
"Water got inside. It made the log rot.	73
Now it is a huge tube.	79
Animals can hide here.	83
They could live in here."	88
"This log is a busy place," said Dan.	96
"This log is food.	100
This log is a home.	105
This log is a place to hide!"	112

© Pearson Education

READ THE SENTENCES

Set A

1. She and her family play soccer.
2. My new hat has three buttons.
3. We saw some cute kittens.
4. They put slippers on their feet.
5. Have you seen my other mitten?
6. Jan keeps rabbits and also sells them.

Set B

1. She and her family play soccer at home.
2. My new hat has three buttons on the top.
3. We saw some cute kittens at the store.
4. They like to have slippers on their feet.
5. Have you seen my other mitten on the shelf?
6. Jan keeps rabbits and also sells them as pets.

Set C

1. She and her family play soccer around the trees.
2. I gave Ned a new hat with three buttons on it.
3. Dee had some cute kittens in a basket.
4. The people had blue slippers on their feet.
5. I have one mitten, but I can't see the other one.
6. Jan keeps rabbits and also takes care of birds.

© Pearson Education

Busy Bees

Have you seen bees buzzing?   5

Bees are busy. They have jobs to do.   13

They keep the hive nice.   18

They find flowers.   21

They also make honey.   25

They are like a family.   30

Some bees hunt for flowers.   35

One bee sees new flowers.   40

It speeds back home. It tells the other bees.   49

Bees can't talk. Bees dance!   54

This bee will dance.   58

The dance is like a map.   64

Other bees come to see.   69

They all go to the flowers.   75

They will get nectar. They will make honey.   83

This is how bees share their jobs.   90

This is how they work together.   96

© Pearson Education

Sentence Reading Chart

Unit 2

	Phonics		High-Frequency		Reteach ✓	Reassess: Words Correct
	Total Words	Words Correct	Total Words	Words Correct		
Week 1 *A Big Fish for Max* A B C						
Digraphs *sh, th*	8					
Vowel Sound in *ball*	7					
High-Frequency Words			7			
Week 2 *The Farmer in the Hat* A B C						
Long *a* (CVCe)	8					
c/s/ and g/j/	9					
High-Frequency Words			7			
Week 3 *Who Works Here?* A B C						
Long *i* (CVCe)	8					
Digraphs *wh, ch, tch*	11					
High-Frequency Words			7			
Week 4 *The Big Circle* A B C						
Long *o* (CVCe)	2					
Contractions *n't, 'm, 'll*	2					
High-Frequency Words			2			
Week 5 *Life in a Forest* A B C						
Long *u*, Long *e* (CVCe)	2					
Inflected Ending -*ed*	2					
High-Frequency Words			2			
Week 6 *Honey Bees* A B C						
Long *e: e, ee*	2					
Syllables VCCV	2					
High-Frequency Words			2			
Unit Scores	**63**		**27**			

- **RECORD SCORES** Use this chart to record scores for the Day 5 Sentence Reading Assessment. Circle A, B, or C to record which set of sentences was used.

- **RETEACH PHONICS SKILLS** If the child is unable to read all the tested phonics words, then reteach the phonics skills using the Reteach lessons on pp. DI·76–DI·84.

- **PRACTICE HIGH-FREQUENCY WORDS** If the child is unable to read all the tested high-frequency words, then provide additional practice for the week's words. See pp. 34e, 62e, 82e, 110e, 136e, and 162e.

- **REASSESS** Use the same set of sentences or an easier set for reassessment.

© Pearson Education

READ THE SENTENCES

Set A

1. He is always happy.
2. We wish for a sunny day.
3. Pam saw nothing go by.
4. She hopes her hat stays dry.
5. Sad things make me cry.
6. Everything becomes so messy.

Set B

1. She tells jokes that are always so funny.
2. No planes will fly on that day next week.
3. We will try to stack things on the shelf.
4. The puppy will be fine if it stays here.
5. She said nothing becomes lost in my house.
6. He made everything in the shop muddy.

Set C

1. He knows it is windy, but nothing should blow away.
2. Things in the house become dusty when we leave the door open.
3. The shy girl always says hi to me in school.
4. We go to a fish fry one day a week.
5. The bunny eats everything she feeds him and still wants more.
6. The sly fox stays so far away that I can't take its picture.

© Pearson Education

Happy Trips

Do you like to go on trips? Do you drive or fly? 12

Trips can be the same in some ways. They will 22
get you where you want to go. You can take a pet 34
like a puppy. If you get sleepy, you can take a nap. 46
The rides can be bumpy too. It can be windy on 57
your trip. The wind can shake you. 64

Flying is a quick way to get where you want to go. 76
You fly in the sky. That is so much fun! 86
You will be on a street when you drive. 95
That is also fun for me. You always 103
see many trucks going fast on the street. 111

© Pearson Education

READ THE SENTENCES

1. Are there enough pancakes for Hank?
2. Can you bring your own backpack?
3. Make sure every cupcake is pink.
4. Any boy can sing by himself.
5. Did you ever skate at an outside rink?
6. The tunes were sung in the daytime.

Set B

1. We were sure the mailbox was by the bank.
2. Frank made his own treehouse in the big tree.
3. I think I put enough sand in the sandbox.
4. They put a jack inside every car trunk.
5. Did you ever see a beehive hang from a tree?
6. Are there any pinecones by the swing?

Set C

1. Make sure you don't ever yank on the little bulldog's leash.
2. Where were the flags that should have hung on the flagpoles?
3. We sang a song before bedtime every night.
4. Did everyone drink enough milk at dinner tonight?
5. She used her own money to buy a ring for herself.
6. Did you see a skunk near any of the houses this weekend?

© Pearson Education

A Bath for Cupcake

Last weekend, Frank gave his dog Cupcake a   8
bath. He could not use the bathtub. And the sink in   19
the shed was too small.   24

Frank got an old pink sandbox. It did not have   34
sand inside. Frank put the sandbox outside on the   43
grass. He filled it with water. Then he picked up   53
Cupcake. He put her into the sandbox. Plunk! She   62
flung water all around. Then she yanked herself   70
from Frank's hands and jumped out.   76

How could Frank get Cupcake to stay in the   85
sandbox? He had to think of something. He gave   94
her a bone. If Cupcake had the bone, she did not   105
jump out of the sandbox. So, everything was fine.   114
Cupcake got her bath.   118

© Pearson Education

READ THE SENTENCES

Set A

1. Jan fixes very good pork.
2. Ben waxes our sports car.
3. Put the glasses and forks away.
4. More buses came to the school.
5. His house has two benches on the porch.
6. Her friends put corn on the dishes.

Set B

1. Sam fishes in the water away from the shore.
2. The old car passes the store on the way home.
3. Dave made a fort with boxes in his house.
4. Our friends wore hats with blue patches on them.
5. A very bad storm made the red foxes hide.
6. Liz watches Ann sort the math papers at school.

Set C

1. Our school has reading classes in the morning and math classes in the afternoon.
2. Dad paid taxes on the car he got in New York.
3. The branches that fell on the house tore a hole in the roof.
4. Mom wishes she could buy a very big boat that is docked at the port.
5. Our friends work at ranches that raise many different kinds of horses.
6. Mack rushes away from the forest when it begins to rain.

© Pearson Education

Morning Chores

Cole and Jess met on Vic's porch one morning.   9
"Can you play ball with us?" asked Cole.   17

"I have chores to do this morning," said Vic. "I   27
have to pick corn. I have to sort my toys. I also   39
have dishes to dry. Next, I have to stack boxes.   49
Then I must pick up branches."   55

"We can help you," said Jess. "We can do all   65
the jobs with you. Then we can play ball.   74

Vic's mother watches the boys as she fixes   82
lunch for them. "How lucky Vic is to have such   92
good friends," she thinks.   96

In no time at all, no more jobs were left. Now   107
they could play ball.   111

© Pearson Education

READ THE SENTENCES

Set A

1. You dropped a few cards.
2. Soon Bill jogged to the barn.
3. How far did Rob get when he stopped?
4. The dog is running in the park again.
5. Meg was getting to be afraid of the dark.
6. It is hard to read sitting in the car.

Set B

1. We soon skipped on the path to the farm.
2. Luke napped as Jack read the paper in the yard.
3. Kim planned to see more than a few stars.
4. Gabe was afraid the glass jar was tipping.
5. How well is Mark hitting the ball when you play?
6. I went shopping for yarn again at the mall.

Set C

1. Clark begged his teacher to read the story again the next day.
2. Soon the dog wagged its tail and started to play with us.
3. Faith grabbed some darts again and began playing another game with Jason.
4. The other fish were afraid of the sharks swimming near them.
5. Mom was knitting, and Mary was playing a few songs on her harp.
6. How long has Maria been clipping charms onto the silver chain?

© Pearson Education

Clark and Star

Clark had a horse named Star. Clark wanted   8
Star to jump. But Star was afraid. Star liked   17
running but not jumping.   21

Every day Clark jogged to the barn. He rode   30
Star all morning. Star trotted around the farm. But 39
he did not jump. Clark patted Star's neck and said, 49
"Good boy. Soon you will jump."   55

One day Clark was humming as he ate figs.   64
"Figs! That is it!" he said.   70

Clark grabbed a bunch of figs. He went to   79
the barn. Clark put the figs on the other side of   90
a rail. Star was a smart horse. To get the figs,   101
he had to jump. So, up he went. Star got the   112
figs. Clark was happy that Star now jumps.   120

© Pearson Education

READ THE SENTENCES

Set A

1. He's done singing his third song.
2. You've got to wait for the clerk.
3. Let's visit the girl at home.
4. They've got to push the herd into the barn.
5. The nurse will know we're here.
6. They're going to visit the shore to surf.

Set B

1. You're first in line to visit the new park.
2. I've got to wait at the birch tree for my friend.
3. She's done with the last term at school.
4. I know there's more perch to catch.
5. We've got to push the car up and turn it around.
6. They know that's the furry bunny they saw in the backyard.

Set C

1. You've got to wait far behind the curb for your ride to school.
2. They're going to wait by the curb for us, and then we will all go to the mall.
3. He's done washing the stain out of his new shirt.
4. Do you know who's going to wear the purple hat at the party?
5. We're going to push her on the swings first.
6. I know it's almost time for the circus to begin.

© Pearson Education

Who's Talking?

Vern had a cat of her own. But she also wanted   11
a bird.   13

"Let's go to the pet store," said Mom.   21

The clerk said, "Here's a bird that can talk."   30

"I've got to have that bird," said Vern.   38

"Sir, we will take the bird on that perch," said   48
Mom.   48

"You're a lucky girl," said the clerk. Vern was   58
happy.   59

"Let's play a trick on Dad," said Vern.   67

When Dad got home, the bird said, "Hi, Dad."   76
Dad turned to look around.   81

"Who's talking?" asked Dad.   85

"That's the cat," said Vern. The cat purred.   93

Then Dad saw a blur fly by. "What's that?"   102

Dad looked at Vern. He said, "You've played a   111
trick on me!" Vern just grinned.   117

© Pearson Education

READ THE SENTENCES

Set A

1. Cut the grass before you trim the thickest hedge.
2. The taller judge said good-bye to us.
3. Does Tad like the sweetest fudge?
4. Oh, the whitest wall has a smudge on it.
5. The bigger wedge of pie is on the right side.
6. You won't want to sit on the tallest ledge.

Set B

1. The larger horse won't walk on the edge of the cliff.
2. Ben and Jade said good-bye to the thinner judge.
3. He ate the freshest cheese wedge before lunch.
4. Oh, the smallest bird sits on the hedge every day.
5. Does the fudge get softer if it is in the sun?
6. Nudge Jake right before it is time for his hike up the shortest hill.

Set C

1. We said the pledge later in the day before the band started playing.
2. Oh, the judge said the skaters were much luckier this year than they were last year.
3. The hedge on the right is the greenest of them all.
4. The smudge won't be seen on the door because it is the darkest color on the house.
5. It was the saddest day of the week as we sat on the ledge and said good-bye.
6. Does this batch of fudge look flatter than the last batch?

© Pearson Education

The Sweetest Yard

Ted fixed up his yard. First, he planted a hedge.   10
This one is greener than the last one. It is also   21
taller. The hedge is on the sunny side of the   31
house.   32

Then, he planted three trees. The largest is in   41
the backyard. The smallest is on one side of the   51
house.   52

Next, he put in roses. These roses are the   61
reddest I have ever seen. They are in the yard   71
by the porch.   74

Last, he dug around the edge of the sidewalk.   83
He put in some plants that grow slower than   92
others.   93

Let's make me the judge. I say Ted's yard is   103
the finest on the block.   108

© Pearson Education

Sentence Reading Chart

Unit 3

	Phonics		High-Frequency		Reteach ✓	Reassess: Words Correct
	Total Words	Words Correct	Total Words	Words Correct		
Week 1 *An Egg Is an Egg* A B C						
Vowel Sounds of *y*	2					
Long Vowels (CV)	2					
High-Frequency Words			2			
Week 2 *Ruby in Her Own Time* A B C						
Final *ng, nk*	2					
Compound Words	2					
High-Frequency Words			2			
Week 3 *Jan's New Home* A B C						
Ending *-es;* Plural *-es*	2					
r-Controlled *or, ore*	2					
High-Frequency Words			2			
Week 4 *Frog and Toad Together* A B C						
Inflected Endings *-ed, -ing*	2					
r-Controlled *ar*	2					
High-Frequency Words			2			
Week 5 *I'm a Caterpillar* A B C						
r-Controlled *er, ir, ur*	2					
Contractions *'s, 've, 're*	2					
High-Frequency Words			2			
Week 6 *Where Are My Animal Friends?* A B C						
Comparative Endings	2					
dge/j/	2					
High-Frequency Words			2			
Unit Scores	24		12			

- **RECORD SCORES** Use this chart to record scores for the Day 5 Sentence Reading Assessment. Circle A, B, or C to record which set of sentences was used.
- **RETEACH PHONICS SKILLS** If the child is unable to read all the tested phonics words, then reteach the phonics skills using the Reteach lessons on pp. DI·76–DI·84.

- **PRACTICE HIGH-FREQUENCY WORDS** If the child is unable to read all the tested high-frequency words, then provide additional practice for the week's words. See pp. 34e, 66e, 90e, 116e, 142e, and 172e.
- **REASSESS** Use the same set of sentences or an easier set for reassessment.

© Pearson Education

READ THE SENTENCES

Set A

1. Nell's mom was surprised that it rained.
2. Jed's dad gives him the mail.
3. Would Ben's train be late?
4. I enjoy playing with the girls' dolls.
5. Do not worry about the cat's tail.
6. Nate's clay art was a surprise.

Set B

1. Would you wait for Pat's call?
2. Jane's main worry was her dog.
3. Nan's card was a surprise to Ray.
4. The shells in our friends' pails surprised us.
5. One day we will worry about the bees' hive.
6. Gail gives us hay from the farmer's barn.

Set C

1. They enjoy the birds' feathers they find on the trail.
2. The workers would like to plant grain in the farmer's field.
3. The students' teacher told them to wait until noon for a surprise.
4. Mom pays for the family's groceries while June gives the bags to Dan.
5. Don't be surprised if the gate's chain breaks.
6. He won't worry about stacking all the teams' trays today.

© Pearson Education

Gail's Dog Runs Away

Rex's tail wagged as he waited for the ball. Ray   10
tossed the ball. Rex got the ball and ran far away.   21

"Oh, no," said Gail. "We have to look for him. It is   33
starting to rain."   36

"Let's go this way," said Ray.   42

They went to Miss Day's house. "Have you seen a   52
gray dog?" asked Gail. "My dog's name is Rex."   61

"No, I haven't seen him," said Miss Day.   69

Then they went to their friends' house. Jay and Kris   79
lived there. "Have you seen Rex?" asked Gail.   87

"Let's look," said Jay.   91

They looked in the boys' yard. There was Rex. He   101
was running with a rabbit and having fun.   109

Gail was happy. It was a good day.   117

© Pearson Education

READ THE SENTENCES

Set A

1. The beads had the prettiest colors.
2. Peg tried to draw a great big seal.
3. Mike drew the silliest beak on the bird.
4. We hurried over to the beach.
5. The sign said they had fried fish to eat.
6. Please show us how you pried the lid off the box.

Set B

1. Fay copied the letters to make a neat sign.
2. Sal dried the leaf with the red and yellow colors.
3. We hurried, and the meal was over fast.
4. Ron spied the box and we each saw the great gift.
5. Peg drew a farm and tried to draw wheat.
6. She will show him the easiest way to draw the sea.

Set C

1. Jen carried the cream to show us she would not spill it.
2. I cried each time I drew a picture of our lost dog.
3. It is easier for our great team to jump over hurdles than it is for theirs.
4. The colors of the leaves this year are prettier than last year.
5. Steve worried that the sea waves could be over his head.
6. Draw a picture of the funniest dream you have ever had.

© Pearson Education

A Day at the Beach

"Mom, may we please go to the beach?" asked   9
Jean.   10

"Help me clean. Then we can go."   17

Jean put her things away. She dusted. She dried   26
the dishes. She put them on the shelf. Jean   35
hurried to get everything done.   40

Then they went to the beach. It was prettier than   50
the last time. The sea was so blue!   58

Jean and her mom walked in the sand. They saw   68
a little seal on a rock. They picked up shells.   78
They picked up sea glass.   83

Jean felt the heat of the sun. This was one of the   95
happiest days of her life.   100

© Pearson Education

READ THE SENTENCES

Set A

1. We took the boat down the stream.
2. I once saw a goat in the street.
3. Don painted wild stripes on the bowl.
4. I found a crow scratching in the dirt.
5. Once Dad had to scrape snow from the window.
6. Joan put a bit of squash in her mouth.

Set B

1. Ted had to scrape the toast before he took a bite.
2. Meg found a brush to scrub the loaf pan.
3. Once I saw a toad on the screen.
4. Show me where Kate found the string.
5. I put a small square of roast beef in my mouth.
6. Mark may spray the box a wild color to make it glow.

Set C

1. A wild animal in the oak tree screeched loudly.
2. Tad took the box and tied it with his own string.
3. In the spring, the logs will flow to the mouth of the river.
4. The goat tripped once and made a big splash in the pond.
5. Zack found some split wood next to the road.
6. We took the street going north along the coast.

© Pearson Education

READ THE STORY

Frogs, Toads, and Fish

I like the spring. My mom and I take walks. We   11
look at the big oak trees. We see the leaves blow   22
in the wind. We look at the yellow roses.   31

We like to go to a little stream. It is down the street   44
from my house. The stream has lots of frogs and   54
toads in it. I like to watch the toads splash in the   66
water. The frogs croak a lot too.   73

One day I saw some fish in the stream. I wanted   84
to show them to my mom. We slowed down to   94
see them. One wild fish splashed water on my   103
new coat.   105

© Pearson Education

READ THE SENTENCES

Set A

1. Eight wrens soared high in the sky.
2. Do not touch the pie or the knife.
3. Jack wrote about the moon at night.
4. The big knot in the tie made me laugh.
5. The knight had a light above the steps.
6. Jan will knit eight bright hats.

Set B

1. I know the fries are too hot to touch.
2. The bands above their wrists were tight.
3. Sue will write about a flight to the moon.
4. Do not laugh at the sight of my wreath.
5. Ken will wrap eight pies.
6. The right knob is above the shelf.

Set C

1. Do not touch the pies in the knapsack.
2. Please wring out the eight wet rags before tonight.
3. You might find the wrens above the light on the porch.
4. The knots in the laces of my right shoe made her laugh.
5. The trees were wrapped in the white light of the moon.
6. Eight wrenches lie on a shelf above the three hammers.

© Pearson Education

A Flight to the Moon

"It is time to eat," said Knob.   7

"Let's go to the moon for lunch," said Wren. "We   17
can go right now. There is a lot of light."   27

Knob and Wren got into their plane. They went   36
high into the sky. It was a great flight.   45

"We are just above the moon. I do not know   55
the way to go," said Knob. He had a knack for   66
getting lost.   68

"Turn right at that beam of light," said Wren.   77
"And do not wreck the plane when you land."   86

Knob and Wren ate fries and pies for lunch.   95
Then they left to go home.   101

"We might be home in time for dinner," said   110
Wren.   111

© Pearson Education

READ THE SENTENCES

Set A

1. His blue backpack is in his room.
2. Ned stood next to his new sandbox.
3. A picture of Sue was in the newspaper.
4. Jill thought she saw a few bluebirds.
5. Remember to put fruit in your lunchbox.
6. The crew thought a rainstorm was coming.

Set B

1. On the cruise, Sam took a picture of the rainbow.
2. Remember to chew the popcorn well.
3. Ron thought he might have grapefruit juice.
4. There is no room for the suit in the knapsack.
5. Nan stood by the campfire as smoke blew the other way.
6. I thought the pen in the wastebasket was a clue.

Set C

1. Glue the picture of the flowerpot in the book.
2. We can play with the new beanbag in my room.
3. Jen did not remember that her homework was due in one day.
4. The baseball hit my leg and gave me a bruise while I stood along first base.
5. Mom thought we could eat stew on the weekend.
6. Did you remember to pack your raincoat and blue suit?

© Pearson Education

Sue Goes Camping

Sue's family went on a camping trip. They had a   10
new blue tent. Sue liked to be outside.   18

One day, Dad and Sue went for a walk. Sue   28
wanted to see a fox. They saw a bluebird. They   38
saw a rabbit. They saw a few snakes. But they did   49
not see a fox. Sue was not happy.   57

At the campfire they ate stew and fruit. Then they   67
had snacks. Mom left a bag of chips on a bench.   78

The next day, the chips were not there. Who took   88
them? Then Sue saw a clue. She saw tracks in the   99
dirt. Sue knew they were fox tracks. But she did   109
not see the fox. "Maybe next time," she thought.   118

© Pearson Education

READ THE SENTENCES

Set A

1. Kate swam across the pool quickly.
2. We were thankful the dance was in a cool room.
3. The tool is useful because it is small.
4. The snoop opened the letter slowly.
5. He only told me about the watchful moose.
6. The loose shoes were colorful.

Set B

1. You can be graceful in shoes or boots.
2. Only a soft broom will clean the tile safely.
3. The dog is playful because it sees its food.
4. We are hopeful the dance will be held at school.
5. She quickly opened the gift and showed me the smooth silk.
6. Rick told us he would gladly be here at noon.

Set C

1. The brightly colored bird swooped across the room.
2. The goose suddenly ran across the yard.
3. I enjoy my weekly visit to dance school.
4. I told her I only wanted one scoop of the flavorful ice cream.
5. We will now have our troop meetings only once a month instead of weekly.
6. The friendly worker opened the gate at the zoo early.

© Pearson Education

Scooter at the Zoo

Last week my mom took me to the zoo because I   11
was helpful around the house. Scooter went too.   19

We got there at noon. "Make sure you stay with   29
us," Mom said to Scooter. Scooter likes to walk   38
away. Maybe that's why we call him Scooter. He   47
scoots around.   49

We walked slowly because we wanted to see   57
everything. We saw playful chimps. The seals   66
were fun to watch in the pool because they are   76
graceful swimmers.   78

"It's time to go home," said Mom. We looked   87
around. Scooter was gone. Soon we found him.   95
He was looking at a moose.   101

"Scooter, you got lost again," said Mom sweetly.   109
"I am not lost," said Scooter bravely. "I thought   118
you were lost." We all smiled and went home.   127

© Pearson Education

Sentence Reading Chart

Unit 4

	Phonics		High-Frequency		Reteach ✓	Reassess: Words Correct
	Total Words	Words Correct	Total Words	Words Correct		
Week 1 *Mama's Birthday Present* A B C						
Long *a: ai, ay*	2					
Possessives	2					
High-Frequency Words			2			
Week 2 *The Dot* A B C						
Long *e: ea*	2					
Inflected Endings	2					
High-Frequency Words			2			
Week 3 *Mister Bones: Dinosaur Hunter* A B C						
Long *o: oa, ow*	2					
Three-Letter Blends	2					
High-Frequency Words			2			
Week 4 *The Lady in the Moon* A B C						
Long *i: ie, igh*	2					
kn/n/ and wr/r/	2					
High-Frequency Words			2			
Week 5 *Peter's Chair* A B C						
Compound Words	2					
Vowels *ew, ue, ui*	2					
High-Frequency Words			2			
Week 6 *Henry and Mudge and Mrs. Hopper's House* A B C						
Suffixes *-ly, -ful*	2					
Vowels in *moon*	2					
High-Frequency Words			2			
Unit Scores	**24**		**12**			

- **RECORD SCORES** Use this chart to record scores for the Day 5 Sentence Reading Assessment. Circle A, B, or C to record which set of sentences was used.
- **RETEACH PHONICS SKILLS** If the child is unable to read all the tested phonics words, then reteach the phonics skills using the Reteach lessons on pp. DI·76–DI·84.

- **PRACTICE HIGH-FREQUENCY WORDS** If the child is unable to read all the tested high-frequency words, then provide additional practice for the week's words. See pp. 42e, 70e, 96e, 124e, 154e, and 186e.
- **REASSESS** Use the same set of sentences or an easier set for reassessment.

© Pearson Education

READ THE SENTENCES

Set A

1. Jan pulled the handle down.
2. The dog had little brown eyes.
3. He never saw a purple crown.
4. Now the turtle is behind the tree.
5. My uncle drove toward town.
6. A single cow walked along the path.

Set B

1. How did the apple get behind the table?
2. The crowd sat along the middle of the track.
3. The clown with the big eyes can juggle.
4. The dogs pulling the sled made a circle and started to howl.
5. The plow rode toward the puddle.
6. The happy girl will giggle but never frown.

Set C

1. Please hang the purple towel behind the door.
2. She pulled the needle through the silk to sew lace on the gown.
3. Jenna saw a mouse wiggle along the brown ledge.
4. The cows moved toward the barn and then huddled together.
5. My dog never growls at my turtle.
6. Owls and eagles have keen eyes that help them find food.

© Pearson Education

Cowboys and Cattle

My uncle is a cowboy. His name is Jud. I went to   12
visit him on his ranch.   17

I rode a brown horse. Her name was Apple.   26
Uncle Jud had a new saddle just for me.   35

Once we went out to check on the cattle. One   45
was missing. We looked behind rocks. We looked   53
down by the stream. We looked along a line of   63
trees. But we could not find the cow.   71

Then we looked in some tall grass. There was   80
the little cow stuck in a mud puddle. Uncle Jud   90
pulled her out with a rope.   96

I want to be a cowboy when I grow up. It is hard   109
work. But it is so much fun!   116

© Pearson Education

READ THE SENTENCES

Set A

1. The pilot loved to fly above the clouds.
2. They eat trout and melon on a wood table.
3. Ned went out the back door of the cabin.
4. We should go south on the river.
5. Amy should have sprouts on her salad.
6. Tulips grew next to the door of the house.

Set B

1. The scout should find the cabin soon.
2. Mike loved the sound of robins in the spring.
3. We should see tiger tracks on the ground.
4. Dave loved the seven baby hounds.
5. The mouse loved to eat bacon.
6. Kim found a wagon outside the door.

Set C

1. The camel loved to sleep on the ground.
2. Ted gave a loud shout when he saw a huge spider on the door.
3. The dragon found some wood to make his home.
4. The robot should clean the couch and the rug.
5. Pete loved the lizard he found on the mound of dirt.
6. The round tower had a door at the bottom.

© Pearson Education

Snout, the Dragon

There was once a dragon. His name was   8
Snout. He lived in a cave, and he was a real   19
grouch. The other animals did not like Snout   27
because he would shout at them when they played.   36

One day Tiger and Camel played kickball.   43
Snout shouted, "Go away!" Fire came out of his   52
mouth. Tiger and Camel ran away.   58

The next day, the lizards played baseball.   65
Snout shouted, "Go away!" Fire came out of his   74
mouth. The lizards ran away.   79

Then a brave mouse jumped on Snout's head   87
and said, "Why are you such a grouch?"   95

Snout said sadly, "The animals do not ask me   104
to play with them."   108

So the animals asked Snout to play with   116
them. Now Snout is not a grouch any more.   125

© Pearson Education

READ THE SENTENCES

Set A

1. Ken likes to read books instead of napping.
2. None of the wood is piled in the shed.
3. The cook is tasting another bit of food.
4. Ty hoped to get another wool scarf.
5. None of the girls took the dancing class.
6. These baked goods are among the best.

Set B

1. Dad used another hook on the door.
2. This book is among the three Steve traded.
3. Tess will be hiking to the brook instead of up the hill.
4. None of the dogs raced to where I stood.
5. The cat is hiding in its nook instead of eating.
6. Look for another skating champ at the rink.

Set C

1. None of them was smiling as they stood still for the picture.
2. Maggie shook another fruit drink and is giving it to Ben.
3. His dancing footwork is among the best there is.
4. Mom liked wood instead of tile for the floor.
5. Jean placed another piece of bait on the fishing hook.
6. A wool sweater is among the clothes that Mom saved.

© Pearson Education

A Good Idea

"It would be great to have a fish tank in our   11
classroom," said Brook.   14

"That would cost a lot," said Miss Woods.   22

"I know what to do. We could pay for the tank   33
by selling cupcakes and cookies," said Marco.   40

So they started making baked goods. The girls   48
baked cupcakes with white icing. The boys baked   56
cookies with green icing. Then they tasted the   64
cupcakes and cookies. Yum! Everything was so   71
good! All the boys and girls liked them.   79

The class got the fish tank they were hoping   88
for. The girls added the plants. The boys put in the   99
fish. Brook and Marco had big smiles on their   108
faces. Miss Woods smiled too.   113

© Pearson Education

READ THE SENTENCES

Set A

1. Joy will be the leader today.
2. What kind of oil did the baker use?
3. The coins from the teller were heavy.
4. Roy goes to see the doctor soon.
5. What kinds of meat did the helper broil?
6. The worker put the toys against the wall.

Set B

1. The driver loaded the heavy soil on the truck.
2. Some readers enjoy many kinds of books.
3. The waiter used a kind of foil to wrap the food.
4. Farmer Ted picked soybeans today.
5. The painter put the moist brushes against the pail.
6. A sailor goes to the boat to join his friends.

Set C

1. The teacher asked Troy how long it would take to move the heavy box to the gym.
2. A kind actor joined the others on stage.
3. The player is loyal to her team and goes to all the games.
4. The horse rider told the boy to put the saddle against the fence.
5. The singer likes joyful kinds of music and encourages everyone to sing with her.
6. Today the worker moved buckets of soil into the garden.

© Pearson Education

King Troy

Troy was a king in a land far away. He did not 12
want to be a king. So he tried to be a sailor. 24

Troy was a good sailor. But he did not get joy 35
from the sea. So he tried to be a farmer. 45

He was a good farmer. But he did not like to 56
work with the soil. So he tried to be a painter. 67

Troy was a good painter. But he got the oil 77
paint all over himself. So he tried to be a banker. 88

He was a good banker. But he did not like to 99
count coins every day. He did not know what to do. 110

The people said, "Come back to the royal family. 119
We want you to be our king." 126

So Troy went home, and he was a great king. 136

© Pearson Education

READ THE SENTENCES

Set A

1. We read about hawks in science class.
2. Paul ate bread early in the day.
3. Ted will learn how to spread the sauce.
4. Pull the thread through the shawl.
5. The pigs built a straw house that was not steady.
6. They saw a play to learn about good health.

Set B

1. Paula is the head of the science club.
2. Can you learn to fix a shawl with thread?
3. The auto's tires were not built with good tread.
4. Kim wanted to draw the meadow early in the day.
5. The science book showed the bird's claws and feathers.
6. Through the trees we could see the head of a fawn.

Set C

1. It is not your fault that the sweater has worn through.
2. Can you haul a case of leather belts to the store early in the morning?
3. Heather reads books to learn about laws.
4. The tractor was built to spread seeds and mow lawns.
5. Science can teach about weather and rocket launches.
6. They ate an early breakfast of eggs and sausage.

© Pearson Education

Blue Threads

Paula looked at her sweater. There were little   8
holes in the arms.   12

"Mom, may I have a shawl for my birthday?   21

"We will see," said Mom.   26

Paula went to her room. She put a straw hat   36
with a feather on her head. "A shawl would look   46
great with this hat," she said to her cat. Muffin just   57
yawned and licked her paw.   62

Every day Paula found little blue threads here   70
and there. "What are these threads?" she said to   79
herself.   80

On her birthday, Paula woke up at dawn.   88
"Happy birthday," said her mom. Paula opened   95
her gift. She saw a soft, blue shawl. Paula's mom   105
knitted it. Paula was not surprised it was blue.   114

"Thanks, Mom." They smiled and hugged   120
each other.   122

© Pearson Education

READ THE SENTENCES

Set A

1. The brothers rebuilt the bike and sold it.
2. Ron is unable to carry the heavy gold.
3. Peg retold most of the story after she answered the door.
4. Where did Ned find the poor unhappy dog?
5. The child had a different way to retie the bow.
6. The kind brothers unpacked the boxes.

Set B

1. Unlock the cage and carry the wild bird.
2. It was a poor place to rebuild the old shed.
3. The brothers told him to unload the truck.
4. I don't mind if you use a different color to repaint the wall.
5. Zack replanted different roses by the post.
6. Hold the baby as I unbutton her coat and then carry her to bed.

Set C

1. The cold weather made it unsafe for the brothers to camp outdoors.
2. I refilled the water bottle while Jill helped us to carry the packs and fold our sleeping bags.
3. Most people answered but were unable to help.
4. The brothers reused the mold to make a vase.
5. Lisa remixed the beans with two different mild sauces.
6. The brothers were unneeded to grind the wheat.

© Pearson Education

Gold

Roy was a poor man. The town was poor too.   10
One day Roy sold his house. He left home to look   21
for gold. He said he would come back and help the   32
town when he was rich.   37

Roy got a mule. He was unable to take much.   47
He walked to a stream. Roy unpacked his mule. He   57
looked but did not find gold. Roy was unhappy.   66

A man told him that most of the gold was over   77
the next hill. He repacked the mule and walked   86
over the hill. He unloaded his mule and went to   96
sleep.   97

The next day, Roy was lucky. He found the   106
most gold he had ever seen! He replaced his mule   116
with a horse and rode home. Roy was rich and   126
kind. He helped the people rebuild the town.   134

© Pearson Education

Sentence Reading Chart

Unit 5

	Phonics		High-Frequency		Reteach ✓	Reassess: Words Correct
	Total Words	Words Correct	Total Words	Words Correct		
Week 1 *Tippy-Toe Chick, Go!* A B C						
Diphthong *ow/ou/*	2					
Syllables C + *le*	2					
High-Frequency Words			2			
Week 2 *Mole and the Baby Bird* A B C						
Diphthong *ou/ou/*	2					
Syllables VCV	2					
High-Frequency Words			2			
Week 3 *Dot and Jabber and the Great Acorn Mystery* A B C						
Vowels in *book*	2					
Inflected Endings	2					
High-Frequency Words			2			
Week 4 *Simple Machines* A B C						
Diphthongs *oi, oy*	2					
Suffixes *-er, -or*	2					
High-Frequency Words			2			
Week 5 *Alexander Graham Bell* A B C						
Vowels *aw, au*	2					
Short *e: ea*	2					
High-Frequency Words			2			
Week 6 *Ben Franklin and His First Kite* A B C						
Prefixes *un-, re-*	2					
Long Vowels *i, o*	2					
High-Frequency Words			2			
Unit Scores	**24**		**12**			

- **RECORD SCORES** Use this chart to record scores for the Day 5 Sentence Reading Assessment. Circle A, B, or C to record which set of sentences was used.
- **RETEACH PHONICS SKILLS** If the child is unable to read all the tested phonics words, then reteach the phonics skills using the Reteach lessons on pp. DI·76–DI·84.

- **PRACTICE HIGH-FREQUENCY WORDS** If the child is unable to read all the tested high-frequency words, then provide additional practice for the week's words. See pp. 42e, 74e, 108e, 138e, 168e, and 202e.
- **REASSESS** Use the same set of sentences or an easier set for reassessment.

© Pearson Education

Monitoring Progress Forms for Grade 2

From *Scott Foresman Reading Street* Teacher's Editions

© Pearson Education

Fluency Progress Chart, Grade 2

Name _____

	1	2	3	4	5	6	7	8	9	10	11	12	13	14	15	16	17	18	19	20	21	22	23	24	25	26	27	28	29	30
125																														
120																														
115																														
110																														
105																														
100																														
95																														
90																														
85																														
80																														
75																														
70																														
65																														
60																														
55																														
50																														
45																														
40																														
35																														
30																														

Timed Reading

© Pearson Education

READ THE SENTENCES

Set A

1. Someone did drop a ring.
2. We will pick up bread at a store somewhere.
3. My friend went to the ice rink.
4. The red bird sings out in the country.
5. I spot a rock by the beautiful house.
6. A girl with a pink hat on her head was in front.

Set B

1. My friend Tom got sick last week.
2. Jim steps in front of the big sink.
3. I think the top of the box is here somewhere.
4. On her head was a beautiful pink hat.
5. Someone will bring bread for lunch.
6. We can pick plums out in the country.

Set C

1. My friend Chuck got a cut on his chin when he slipped on the stick.
2. The breakfast milk dripped down the front of her dress.
3. Dead leaves hang from the tree in the country.
4. Meg wanted someone to bring watermelons back.
5. He lives somewhere on that block.
6. The beautiful sunset in the west took Frank's breath away.

© Pearson Education

The New Friend

Jack walked slowly home from school. "Why do   8
we have to live here, anyway?" he grumbled.   16

This had been Jack's third day at his new   25
school. It was the same every day. No one said   35
anything to Jack. Everyone had their own friends.   43
He wished that he had someone to eat lunch with.   53
Jack counted cracks in the sidewalk on his way   62
home. "Watch out!" a girl said. "You almost walked   71
right into me!"   74

She looked at him. "My name is Ming. I saw you   85
in school. Do you live on this block?"   93

Jack was shocked that she talked to him. "Yes,"   102
he said. "My house is around the corner."   110

The girl nodded her head. "I live on the next   120
street. I'm meeting my friend Frank. We're going to   129
play soccer. Want to come?"   134

"Sure!" Jack said. "This place isn't so bad after   143
all."   144

© Pearson Education

READ THE SENTENCES

Set A

1. The wise woman had lace on her dress.
2. Those machines move things.
3. That page shows the age of the woman.
4. Nice people live by that gate.
5. Work with a pencil in that space.
6. Roses grow everywhere in the city.

Set B

1. The sun rose as I drove to work.
2. We live by a nice ice rink.
3. My mom works at a place where lace is made.
4. The woman gave me a case of fake gems.
5. There is a huge machine in that place.
6. Those men moved the garbage.

Set C

1. I want to race in places all around the world.
2. Many people like to live in big cities.
3. Some people ride a train to work in the city.
4. The woman ran a fast race through the village.
5. Huge machines move big blocks of stone.
6. The wise woman teaches me how to make fine lace.

© Pearson Education

Going into Space

Do you want to go to new places? Do you like fast   12
rides? If you said yes to all these things, then you   23
can go into space. Some people who went into   32
space began planning for it when they were your   41
age. You can too.   45

You will need go to school for a long time. You   56
will need to know about math. You will need to   66
know about the sun and the stars.   73

Before you go into space, you will find out how   83
machines in space work. You will know what to do if   94
something goes wrong. You might even take along   102
some mice to see how they do in space.   111

Who knows? Maybe one day you will pose in a   121
spacecraft for the news on TV!   127

© Pearson Education

READ THE SENTENCES

Set A

1. The old black bear couldn't run very fast.
2. I love to ride over the bump on that bridge.
3. Let's build a tree house near the nest.
4. My mother told me to drink my milk.
5. Does your father have flowers in the yard?
6. Trot straight down that street.

Set B

1. He couldn't write with the blue ink.
2. Tom loves to swim and jump in the water.
3. Brad will help build a green doghouse.
4. My mother drives a big truck.
5. My father got a blue shirt from my mother.
6. The bear went straight to the big tree.

Set C

1. Kent couldn't stop himself as he coasted down the hill.
2. I love spring when the flowers bloom and look fresh and perfect.
3. It wasn't my dad's fault that he couldn't start to build my tree house that day.
4. My mother kept all my drawings from first grade.
5. Your father has my grandfather's old belt tied around his waist.
6. To get to Big Bear Camp, head straight down Spring Street.

© Pearson Education

A World in the City

Grace and Trent were twins who lived in a | 9
skyscraper in a huge city. One day their mother's | 18
sister Chris came over to visit. | 24

"How is school going?" she asked. | 30

"We're reading about exploring the world," | 36
Grace said. "We found out about stars." | 43
"But Grace and I can't explore the world," Trent | 52
said. "We have to stay right here in this place." | 62

Chris said, "Well, you have trees in the city. | 71
We have birds, and we have the sky. We also | 81
have flowers growing in the front yard. And most | 90
of all, we have the lake!" | 96

She went over to the big window. "Tell me what | 106
you see from here." | 110

"I see the sun and waves and the beach, and I | 121
also see some small clouds," said Grace. | 128

"Oh, I get it!" Trent said. "We can explore the | 138
world right outside our window!" | 143

© Pearson Education

READ THE SENTENCES

Set A

1. The water in the lake looks beautiful.
2. I shaded my eyes from the sun.
3. My dad and I will go visiting early.
4. We petted some animals at the farm.
5. We showed Mom the pail that is full of nuts.
6. I wanted a warm coat.

Set B

1. Are you getting a glass of water?
2. He was rubbing his eyes.
3. He likes to get up early.
4. Animals are living in that tree.
5. We are getting a box that is full of paper.
6. It was warm when we were walking.

Set C

1. Please water the flowers if they are drooping or dropping.
2. My sister closes her eyes when she sneezes.
3. Getting to school early leaves us time to play.
4. Tim loves animals and takes good care of them.
5. The teacher stopped and jumped on the bus that was full of kids.
6. A warm day makes people everywhere think of going outside and taking it easy.

© Pearson Education

A Walk in the Woods

Early this morning, my mom, dad and I went for   10
a walk in the woods. Everywhere we walked, we   19
liked what we saw.   23

It had rained the night before. Water hung on the   33
tree leaves. Little showers sprinkled us when we   41
brushed by them.   44

Suddenly I saw something out of the corner of my   54
eye. I jumped back in surprise. Dad poked the grass   64
with a stick. It was a little green snake.   73

"You don't need to be afraid of this little thing,"   83
Dad said. He picked it up and showed it to me. I   95
though it was cute.   99

"Can we take it home?" I asked.   106

"No, it won't make a good pet," Mom said.   115

I couldn't take the snake home, but I did take   125
home some red leaves. When I look at them, I will   136
think about that beautiful warm day and our walk in   146
the woods.   148

© Pearson Education

READ THE SENTENCES

Set A

1. Put the pieces of cloth together.
2. That chart is very big.
3. Garth said I can learn to fish.
4. His shirts often fit me.
5. It looks as though the wheel broke.
6. My watch is gone!

Set B

1. We can fix this thing together.
2. Look at that bunch of very big pieces.
3. I wish I could learn to play the flute.
4. The dog often wants to go with me.
5. I'll go there, though I don't want to.
6. Where have they gone?

Set C

1. Let's go to the show together.
2. I'll be very happy if you choose those pieces.
3. Can the baby learn to catch a ball?
4. Mothers often sit on that bench in the park.
5. The bag at home base should be white, though it looks pretty dirty now.
6. The chocolate chip cookies are all gone.

© Pearson Education

Little Bear

Little Bear looked at the beautiful, huge tree.   8
"Mom said I can learn to go up there," she said   19
to herself. "I think I can do it if I just reach for the   33
right branch."   35

She watched a white bird fly into the tree.   44
"I wish I could fly straight up there. But I know   55
just thinking about that won't make it happen,"   63
Little Bear said.   66

"What are you waiting for?" the white bird   74
asked. "Bears everywhere in the world have gone   82
up trees. Just do it!"   87

So Little Bear started up, but then she   95
stopped. "I'm too short!" she said.   101

"No, you are not," the bird said. "You just have   111
to try, try, and try again."   117

"I'll just grit my teeth and do it," Little Bear said.   128
So she tried. And she fell. She tried and   137
she fell. She tried and she fell again. Then   146
she tried one last time.   151

And there she was, sitting on the branch.   159
"I learned to do it!" Little Bear said.   167

© Pearson Education

Sentence Reading Chart

Unit 1

	Phonics		High-Frequency		Reteach ✓	Reassess: Words Correct
	Total Words	Words Correct	Total Words	Words Correct		
Week 1 *Iris and Walter* A B C						
Short Vowels; *ea/e/*	4					
High-Frequency Words			2			
Week 2 *Exploring Space with an Astronaut* A B C						
Long Vowels CVCe; *c/s/, g/j/, s/z/*	4					
High-Frequency Words			2			
Week 3 *Henry and Mudge and the Starry Night* A B C						
Consonant Blends	4					
High-Frequency Words			2			
Week 4 *A Walk in the Desert* A B C						
Inflected Endings *-s, -ed, -ing*	4					
High-Frequency Words			2			
Week 5 *The Strongest One* A B C						
Consonant Digraphs	4					
High-Frequency Words			2			
Unit Scores	20		10			

- **RECORD SCORES** Use this chart to record scores for the Day 5 Sentence Reading Assessment. Circle A, B, or C to record which set of sentences was used.
- **RETEACH PHONICS SKILLS** If the child is unable to read all the tested phonics words, then reteach the phonics skills using the Reteach lessons on pp. DI·64–DI·68.

- **PRACTICE HIGH-FREQUENCY WORDS** If the child is unable to read all the tested high-frequency words, then provide additional practice for the week's words. See pp. 40e, 66e, 94e, 126e, and 156e.
- **REASSESS** Use the same set of sentences or an easier set for reassessment.

© Pearson Education

READ THE SENTENCES

Set A

1. My family went to a large farm.
2. I heard a dog bark from the north.
3. Once we saw corn by the barn.
4. Pull the cord before you go.
5. Listen to Carl give the order.
6. Art did not break his arm.

Set B

1. Barb said, "Once I went to see Martin."
2. I will have a party with my large family.
3. You must listen and do each chore in the army.
4. He heard me tell corny jokes to Mr. Marshall.
5. Did you see the farmer pull the short, fat pig in?
6. Do not break the vase with the border because I adore it.

Set C

1. Once they made the formula, they sold a portion.
2. It is an ordinary day, because I did not take a break from my boring work.
3. Listen and do not ignore me, or you will make things much harder.
4. The superstar will come and perform the songs for my family.
5. I heard him inform you that the artwork will go on sale in a day or two.
6. The gardener will pull up weeds by the ballpark.

© Pearson Education

Bart's Problem

Carla sat on the porch with her artwork. 8

"Do you want to help me pick corn?" asked Mom. 18

"Yes, I can help you with that chore," said Carla. 28

"It may storm so we need to be quick!" said Mom. 39

"We can walk past that flower border and go
to the barn." 51

"May I ride Bart from the barn to the field?" asked
Carla. 63

"That is not the best idea," said Mom. 71

"But Bart is a fast horse, and he can run farther
than the others." 85

"I do not think that is smart, Carla. There is sort of
a problem," said Mom. 101

"Bart can take us to the field before the storm hits,"
said Carla. 114

"I do not want to alarm you, but Bart cannot help,"
said Mom with a smile. "Bart has a bad habit. He
likes to eat corn!" 140

"Oh, that is not the kind of help we need!"
said Carla. 152

© Pearson Education

READ THE SENTENCES

Set A

1. He's funny, but Joan didn't laugh.
2. We'll see if there's a great place to park.
3. I'm glad you're happy and aren't sad.
4. He'll either be here by noon, or he isn't coming.
5. She'll find out if they'll be in second place.
6. It certainly wasn't the worst game that she'll play.

Set B

1. Kim's first in line, but who's second?
2. It's certainly the worst storm she's seen.
3. Mom doesn't laugh when the room isn't clean.
4. He'll be a great help if the work hasn't been done.
5. Here's when I'll have to know if you're staying with us.
6. There's either juice or milk that's here to drink.

Set C

1. The great big hill wasn't easy to climb up, and it can't be hard to get down.
2. They'll either go on a picnic, or I'll meet them at the zoo on Friday.
3. I'm sure you'll laugh when you see how funny the show is.
4. It's certainly the worst trip that we'll ever make.
5. She's a great friend, when I don't know what to do.
6. That's the second letter that he's written to his pen pal in China.

© Pearson Education

Dora Can't Skate

Dora put on her skates and stepped on the ice.   10
"This isn't going to work," she said to her friend   20
Amy. "I'll never learn to skate."   26

"You'll have to let go of the rail," said Amy.   36

"I'll fall if I let go. I'm just too scared." Then   47
Dora's brother glided past her. "He's such a good   56
skater," said Dora.   59

"Let go of the rail," he said as he zoomed by   70
Dora.   71

Then Dora saw a lady helping other skaters.   79
"Who's that?" Dora asked.   83

"She's a skating teacher. I'm sure she'll help   91
you. Let's ask her," said Amy.   97

"You'll have to let go of the rail if you want to   109
learn to skate," she said.   114

Dora tried to be brave. She let go and began   124
to glide around the ice. She did fall, but it wasn't   135
so bad. "I'm a skater!" she said to herself.   144

"I guess I can't hold on to things that aren't going   155
to help."   157

© Pearson Education

READ THE SENTENCES

Set A

1. The girl ate enough perch for lunch.
2. The bird and turtle walked toward the pond.
3. What is the first word on her list?
4. The whole herd was in the third pen.
5. Dad fixed the curb by the fir tree a long time ago.
6. The surf was above Kirk's head.

Set B

1. The dog's whole head was full of curly fur.
2. Plant the fern toward the curve of the garden.
3. The robin chirped in the birch tree above us.
4. The nurse lost her purse and hat a long time ago.
5. Stir the pancake batter enough, but do not hurry.
6. She tried to offer a kind word to her hurt friend.

Set C

1. Have they served enough water to drink, or are you still thirsty?
2. We walked toward the clerk who was behind the shirt counter.
3. The teacher said to turn the paper over and write one spelling word in the circle.
4. A long time ago, the circus came to our city and set up a huge purple tent.
5. The river rose above its banks and flooded the church with swirling water.
6. Dad cooked a whole turkey with stuffing and didn't burn it!

© Pearson Education

The Purple Shirt

Fox and Turkey sat in the sun and waited for   10
Turtle. "What do you want for your birthday?"   18
asked Fox when he saw Turtle.   24

"I would like a purple shirt," said Turtle. "I do   34
not like my dark green shell. You have red fur,   44
Fox. And your feathers are beautiful, Turkey.   51
Purple is better than any other color."   58

Later, Fox and Turkey went to a little pond.   67
First, they got purple plums and mashed them up.   76
They put the plums in the water. Next, they put the   87
shirt in and stirred it up. They left the shirt in the   99
pond so it would turn purple.   105

Before long, Turtle came to the pond. It was a   115
hot day, so he went for a swim.   123

The next day, Turtle asked, "Did you get me a   133
purple shirt?"   135

Fox and Turkey looked at him and laughed.   143
"You do not need a purple shirt! You are purple!"   153

Turtle was not upset. He loved it! He was the   163
only purple turtle in the whole woods!   170

© Pearson Education

READ THE SENTENCES

Set A

1. The sign said there were dogs and kitties for sale.
2. Shall we dry the glasses and dishes?
3. There are probably pennies and dimes on the shelf.
4. The roses and pansies had a pleasant smell.
5. The bunnies were scared of the cats.
6. Most people bought lunches in boxes.

Set B

1. The people on the stages sang pleasant tunes.
2. Jane used brushes to paint the letters on the sign.
3. Shall I read stories to the classes?
4. Mike bought kites to fly on the beaches.
5. We will probably ride buses in the cities.
6. The thunder scared the horses and puppies.

Set C

1. Some people will probably ride mules into the canyon, but others will hike.
2. Our families enjoyed a pleasant day of picking peaches at the farm.
3. Shall we make copies of all the pages for everybody?
4. At the fair, Dad bought ice cream cones and slices of watermelon for us to eat.
5. The sign told us that the paint on the benches and swings was still wet.
6. A snake scared Aunt Barb while we were planting daisies and lilies.

© Pearson Education

Animal Wishes

Owl asked all his friends to gather together.   8
"Now that summer is almost here, I would like to   18
know what your wishes are."   23

"Bees, what do you wish for?" Owl asked.   31

"We wish for lots of pansies and other flowers.   40
We can make honey for other animals and build   49
big hives."   51

"Turtles, what do you wish for?" Owl asked.   59

"We wish for lots of rain. The rain will fill the   70
ponds and lakes. Then all the animals will have   79
water to drink. And we will have places to swim."   89

"Birds, what do you wish for?" Owl asked.   97

"We wish for lots of berry bushes. Then all the   107
birds will have plenty of berries to eat. We will   117
chirp all day. The animals like to listen to birds   127
chirping."   128

Then one little bird asked, "What is your wish,   137
Owl?"   138

Owl said, "I wish all of your wishes come true."   148

© Pearson Education

READ THE SENTENCES

Set A

1. Mark brought the mail and paper inside.
2. Everybody was sorry Jay couldn't stay longer.
3. We will wait by the trail for one more minute.
4. I promise to clean the tray before I play.
5. Do not put hay away behind the barn door.
6. A chain keeps the main door shut.

Set B

1. Bess brought the gray sand pail to the beach.
2. The train may be here any minute now.
3. We promise to make you a plain vase from the clay later.
4. Ray was sorry he didn't pay the bill on time.
5. Hang the apron on the nail behind the door.
6. Which way did everybody go after class today?

Set C

1. We promise to call and say hello the minute we sail into town.
2. The clouds brought so much rain that all the grain got soaked.
3. We are sorry we could not paint the fence, but we will do it in April.
4. The maid sprayed the room and closed the door when she was finished cleaning.
5. Everybody in the club will fly to Spain for a holiday trip.
6. Jada's dog strayed from behind her home.

The Day of the Mermaid

Gail and her brother David lived in a plain   9
house on a plain street. Each day was the same   19
for Gail. She wanted something different.   25

She could not wait for the big family trip. They   35
were going far away. Later that week, they took a   45
train to a lake. Then the family went sailing. Gail   55
looked into the water. "I can see a mermaid," she   65
said to David.   68

"You do not. There are no such things as   77
mermaids," said David. David saw a sad look in   86
Gail's eyes. So he decided to play along with the   96
game and put some excitement into the trip. "I   105
can see a whale that's 50 feet long!"   113

"I see it too," Gail said with glee. "Now I see a   125
squid with 20 arms! It's right next to a huge snail."   136

Gail and David laughed as they made up things   145
they saw in the water. Gail was having an amazing   155
day. And it was different from all the rest.   164

© Pearson Education

Name _____

Sentence Reading Chart Unit 2

	Phonics		High-Frequency		Reteach ✓	Reassess: Words Correct
	Total Words	Words Correct	Total Words	Words Correct		
Week 1 _Tara and Tiree, Fearless Friends_ A B C						
_r_-Controlled _ar, or, ore:_ Syllables VCCV	4					
High-Frequency Words			2			
Week 2 _Ronald Morgan Goes to Bat_ A B C						
Contractions _n't, 's, 'll, 'm_	4					
High-Frequency Words			2			
Week 3 _Turtle's Race with Beaver_ A B C						
_r_-Controlled _er, ir, ur:_ Syllables VCCV	4					
High-Frequency Words			2			
Week 4 _The Bremen Town Musicians_ A B C						
Plurals _-s, -es, -ies_	4					
High-Frequency Words			2			
Week 5 _A Turkey for Thanksgiving_ A B C						
Long _a: a, ai, ay;_ Syllables VCV	4					
High-Frequency Words			2			
Unit Scores	20		10			

- **RECORD SCORES** Use this chart to record scores for the Day 5 Sentence Reading Assessment. Circle A, B, or C to record which set of sentences was used.
- **RETEACH PHONICS SKILLS** If the child is unable to read all the tested phonics words, then reteach the phonics skills using the Reteach lessons on pp. DI·64–DI·68.

- **PRACTICE HIGH-FREQUENCY WORDS** If the child is unable to read all the tested high-frequency words, then provide additional practice for the week's words. See pp. 188e, 216e, 250e, 280e, and 310e.
- **REASSESS** Use the same set of sentences or an easier set for reassessment.

© Pearson Education

READ THE SENTENCES

Set A

1. Jake keeps sheep in the village.
2. He planted seeds in science class.
3. Ann cleaned her muddy shoe.
4. Can you guess which team won the jeep?
5. It's fun to watch the baby eagles.
6. There are pretty trees on my street.

Set B

1. We will read about streams in our science books.
2. I guess he had a good reason to sleep so late.
3. Sandy won a blue ribbon for her peach pie.
4. A pretty creek runs behind the village park.
5. The weak heel on my black shoe broke off.
6. Watch the little seals leap into the water.

Set C

1. Miss Beech will teach us about rain and sleet in science class today.
2. My buddy lives in a village near the rocky beach.
3. A lady left a pretty green shoe in a locker at the gym.
4. She was eager to find out who won the track meet at her school.
5. Can you guess who will give the best speech this week?
6. I even like to watch the wheat sway in the breeze down on the farm.

© Pearson Education

Sailing the Sea

A buddy asked me if I would like to go sailing 11
on the sea. I was eager to go. My dream was to 23
see at least one whale. 28

We planned to leave in the summer. It seemed 37
like a long time, but the day came for us to depart. 49
I was happy. Before we left, we packed enough 58
food to last for a week. We would have to fix all of 71
our meals on the boat. 76

It was so great to feel the sea breeze. We saw 87
many kinds of fish. We even saw seals jumping off 97
huge rocks into the deep water. 103

On the third day, I got the treat of my life. We 115
saw three whales leap out of the water. I 124
screamed with joy. 127

When we reached shore at the end of the 136
week, I was ready to put my feet on dry land. But I 149
hope I can sail on the sea next summer. 158

© Pearson Education

READ THE SENTENCES

Set A

1. The old road led to faraway places.
2. We had no company on the boat.
3. Put the answer below the first row.
4. Use soap to wash the roasting pan.
5. Joan's parents sold their house.
6. Show the school picture to the coach.

Set B

1. His parents stayed at the motel on the coast.
2. We can wash most of the oak desks at school.
3. Snow was on top of the faraway frozen pond.
4. Our company wore wool coats in the cold weather.
5. I took a picture of the goat eating oats.
6. Cody almost told the teacher the wrong answer.

Set C

1. Her parents told her to mow the grass after she came home from school.
2. Their company stayed at the only open hotel in town.
3. Jose got bonus points for the answer he wrote about how coal was mined.
4. Logan's school is faraway from the post office.
5. Colin took a picture of a crow in a field next to a black foal.
6. You must first soak the wood with foamy water and then wash the mold off.

© Pearson Education

Goby the Goat

There was once an old goat named Goby. He   9
had spent his life eating green grass. Goby would   18
roam from field to field to locate the best grass on   29
which to munch.   32

One day Goby stopped eating. He had eaten so   41
much grass, he could not eat another bite. Logan   50
was Goby's owner. Logan was very upset because   58
Goby stopped eating. The vet told Logan to try   67
giving Goby other food.   71

Sometimes Logan would take Goby oats in a   79
bowl. Other times Logan might throw him a tomato   88
or a potato. He even tried giving him fruit. Goby   98
just gave a groan and turned up his nose.   107

One day Logan gave him a piece of his leftover   117
toast. It had a little butter and jam on it. Goby   128
tasted the toast. Yum, yum! It was the most he   138
had eaten in a long time. From that day on, Goby   149
ate only toast with butter and jam. That made   158
Logan happy too.   161

© Pearson Education

READ THE SENTENCES

Set A

1. Make whatever kind of homemade cupcakes you would like.
2. I got a postcard today from my grandmother.
3. We will finally get the goldfish sometime tomorrow.
4. Hailey caught a grasshopper in the backyard.
5. I believe Jason made the snowman himself.
6. Meg has been looking for seashells and starfish.

Set B

1. Today, we watched a tugboat from the riverbank.
2. I believe that Kim and Ned have been playing basketball in the driveway.
3. The sunshine finally came out after the rainstorm.
4. Choose whatever wristwatch you want for your birthday.
5. The sailboat got caught on a sandbar.
6. Tomorrow we will eat buttermilk pancakes.

Set C

1. I believe he caught the baseball in the outfield.
2. Whatever happened to the flashlight Dad bought at the drugstore?
3. The airplane finally took off after sitting on the runway for twenty minutes.
4. We couldn't play volleyball today because there was a downpour that flooded the court.
5. My aunt will serve oatmeal and applesauce tomorrow morning.
6. The fruitcake has been in the cupboard since November.

© Pearson Education

Snowstorm Fun

Sometimes when there is a big snowstorm,   7
there is no school. On these snow days, Mom has   17
to call a babysitter. I like it when my babysitter is   28
my grandmother because she enjoys baking.   34

She likes to make homemade bread or   41
cupcakes. They are so delicious! Grandma lets me   49
mix things in big bowls.   54

In the afternoon, I go outside to play. That's   63
when the real fun begins. I have to bundle up in   74
my coat, scarf, hat, and boots because it is so cold   85
outside. I always put on mittens so I do not get   96
frostbite. But I do like to feel the snowflakes on   106
my face.   108

My friend Emma and I play in the backyard.   117
We like to jump into the snowdrifts! Then we roll   127
huge balls of snow to make a snowman.   135
Sometimes we can't put the head on because it is   145
too tall to reach. So my brother helps us. I like   156
these snow days because they are so much fun!   165

© Pearson Education

READ THE SENTENCES

Set A

1. What kind of pie did you buy?
2. My daughters might try to skate.
3. Half of the lights are too bright.
4. We saw many stars in the night sky.
5. The pilot will fly alone today.
6. Their youngest child started to cry.

Set B

1. Many plants died due to the high heat.
2. Half of the dried spices tasted mild.
3. The youngest girl was silent during the flight.
4. The spy didn't mind eating alone.
5. Their daughters tried to fry eggs for lunch.
6. Please buy peach pies to eat tonight after dinner.

Set C

1. I will grind the walnuts and chop half of the dried fruit to put into the cookies.
2. Their two youngest daughters are shy and might be frightened by the scary masks.
3. Spiders stay out of sight as they try to catch insects in their webs.
4. The mild weather was just right for many people to go bike riding.
5. Tyler will buy a bright tie to wear on Friday.
6. The tiger hid behind the tree but was not alone in the forest.

© Pearson Education

A Tiger at Night   2.37

Tiger woke up from a nap. "I'm hungry," he   9
thought. "I should find some food tonight."   16

Tiger saw a wild pig. "That pig would make a   26
yummy dinner. But she is far away, and I do no feel   38
like running after her. I'll rest now and look for food   49
later."   50

Tiger didn't know it, but the wild pig saw him.   60
She was a kind pig. "I'd better tell my friends that   71
the sly tiger is looking for his dinner." But she was   82
too frightened to go, and she cried.   89

A tiny bird flew out from behind a tree and said,   100
"You hide. I'll fly through the forest and tell the   110
other animals." The other animals were sure that   118
the bird did not lie, so they hid out of sight.   129

After Tiger woke up, he was hungry and   137
started to hunt. The night was silent, and Tiger   146
could not find one animal. He thought, "Why didn't   155

I run after that wild pig when I saw it?" So Tiger   167
went hungry that night.   171

© Pearson Education

READ THE SENTENCES

Set A

1. Her clothes were cleaner and whiter than mine.
2. Her only question was the shortest and wisest.
3. Sooner or later Ted will save enough money.
4. Our neighbors have the smoothest but muddiest yard.
5. Morgan taught me to use sweeter, milder spices.
6. We dug in the flattest, dustiest dirt for hours.

Set B

1. Mr. Mills asked a newer and harder question.
2. The tallest, greenest tree cost more money.
3. My clothes got wetter and messier as it rained.
4. He rode the bumpiest, longest trail for hours.
5. My only day off was the coldest, windiest day.
6. My neighbors taught me to use sharper, finer pencils.

Set C

1. The answer to each question taught us how to be healthier and happier.
2. We wore light clothes on the hottest, sunniest day.
3. Ed spent hours climbing the largest, bumpiest hill.
4. The fanciest kite that flew the highest cost the most money.
5. Ashley's neighbors have hair that is curlier and redder.
6. Maria prefers only the softer, thicker blanket.

© Pearson Education

The Smartest Way Down
2.50

Paige and Kayla were hiking one day. The girls always felt healthier and happier outside when they were in the warm sun. But the hiking was hard because this was the rockiest, bumpiest trail on the hill.

Kayla tried to find a flatter path but didn't. They got to the top and stopped for lunch because they were hungrier and thirstier than ever before. No sooner were they rested then it was time to start back down the hill.

A little rain made the trail muddier than it had been before. So they took a different path and had to walk slower. It was the steepest part. Paige said they could fall if they tried to carry their backpacks. So she rigged up some ropes. Kayla lowered the backpacks to Paige and then hiked down.

Paige told Kayla that the idea was the smartest one of the whole trip. Kayla thought that was the nicest thing Paige could have said.

9
16
26
34
37

47
57
65
75
79

89
99
108
118
126
134
135

143
152
160

© Pearson Education

Sentence Reading Chart

Unit 3

	Phonics		High-Frequency		Reteach ✔	Reassess: Words Correct
	Total Words	Words Correct	Total Words	Words Correct		
Week 1 *Pearl and Wagner: Two Good Friends* A B C						
Long *e: e, ee, ea, y;* Syllables VCV	4					
High-Frequency Words			2			
Week 2 *Dear Juno* A B C						
Long *o: o, oa, ow;* Syllables VCV	4					
High-Frequency Words			2			
Week 3 *Anansi Goes Fishing* A B C						
Compound Words	4					
High-Frequency Words			2			
Week 4 *Rosa and Blanca* A B C						
Long *i: i, ie, igh, y*	4					
High-Frequency Words			2			
Week 5 *A Weed Is a Flower* A B C						
Comparative Endings	4					
High-Frequency Words			2			
Unit Scores	**20**		**10**			

- **RECORD SCORES** Use this chart to record scores for the Day 5 Sentence Reading Assessment. Circle A, B, or C to record which set of sentences was used.
- **RETEACH PHONICS SKILLS** If the child is unable to read all the tested phonics words, then reteach the phonics skills using the Reteach lessons on pp. DI·64–DI·68.

- **PRACTICE HIGH-FREQUENCY WORDS** If the child is unable to read all the tested high-frequency words, then provide additional practice for the week's words. See pp. 342e, 370e, 400e, 424e, and 458e.
- **REASSESS** Use the same set of sentences or an easier set for reassessment.

© Pearson Education

READ THE SENTENCES

Set A

1. The quilt had an apple in a circle.
2. Mom had a bundle of stuffing on the table.
3. Jane wrapped the little rattles with paper.
4. Don pretended he was able to play a bugle.
5. We found old bottles and candles in the trunks.
6. Uncle Ron unpacked the purple blankets.

Set B

1. Are you able to handle the old trunks without me?
2. Gail made little stitches with a needle on the quilt.
3. Uncle Ted put apple stuffing into the large turkey.
4. Kyle wrapped the bottles of pickles with ribbons.
5. Ned pretended to be on a cattle drive and put saddle blankets on the horses.
6. Grace unpacked the bundle that was on the table.

Set C

1. Emma tumbled to the ground and dropped the blankets in a mud puddle.
2. The girls giggled with joy as they unpacked the toys and puzzles from the trunks.
3. Logan wiggled as the doctor wrapped his ankle.
4. Juan put his pet turtle in the middle of the yard and pretended it was a giant lizard.
5. The quilt had a design with a single eagle in the center and stars surrounding it.
6. We huddled around the table as Mom made chestnut stuffing for the turkey.

© Pearson Education

Jingle and Jangle

Jingle and Jangle were two horses. Jingle lived   8
on a cattle ranch on the north side of the fence,   19
and Jangle lived on the south side.   26

Jingle and Jangle were about the same size.   34
When they were little, they both liked to race along   44
the fence. They also ate the green apples that fell   54
on each side of the fence.   60

The two horses were different in some ways.   68
Jingle was brown with white down the middle of   77
her face. Jangle was all black. Unlike Jangle,   85
Jingle was able to jump small hedges. Jingle didn't   94
mind having a saddle on her back, but Jangle   103
didn't like a saddle. He would wiggle and kick   112
a lot.   114

One day Jingle was sold to another rancher.   122
Jangle lost the sparkle in his eye. He missed his   132
pal. Then Jangle was sold. When he got to his   142
new ranch, there was Jingle, running and   149
jumping. They were happy once again. They   156
huddled together and ate green apples.   162

© Pearson Education

READ THE SENTENCES

Set A

1. Look at all the good fruit that we will harvest.
2. Can you pull out the root of the bush?
3. He stood on soil by the brook.
4. Push the vine away from the pile of wood.
5. I put my foot on the bumpy road.
6. The book slid off the smooth shelf in the nook.

Set B

1. We put fruit in a pot and cooked it to make jam.
2. I took a step, and my foot slid on the smooth tile.
3. Jack shook the soil off of the root of the bush.
4. A bull walked down the bumpy path to drink from the brook.
5. Our baskets were full of good corn at harvest time.
6. Meg stood by the vine and looked at the bunches of grapes.

Set C

1. The crook wearing a hood slipped on the smooth bricks as he tried to run away.
2. Please put some fruit in the pudding for dessert.
3. We found the footprint of a deer in the soil by the brook.
4. Hang the vine on the hook in the nook next to the kitchen.
5. Carrots are orange, bumpy, root vegetables that taste very good when you cook them.
6. We push a cart full of vegetables that we harvest.

© Pearson Education

Corn Is Good!

Did you know that corn was served at the first   10
Thanksgiving? But it's even older than that.   17
Kernels that are almost 4,000 years old have   25
been found in caves.   29

Today people still eat corn. It is the best grain   39
that can be grown. Corn is so good! I think most   50
people like to eat corn. Some animals eat   58
corn too.   60

Corn comes in many colors. The kernels can   68
look yellow, white, red, or blue. I think white corn is   79
the sweetest. If you took a bite, you would love it!   90

Take a look in a cookbook. You can find many   100
ways to cook sweet corn. You can cook it in water   111
and eat it right off the cob. I eat two before I get   124
full. You can make corn bread or creamed corn.   133
You might try cooking cobs over a wood fire when   143
you camp. Pull the leaves back and dig in. That's   153
the best way to eat corn. And don't forget   162
popcorn. Everybody likes popcorn.   166

© Pearson Education

READ THE SENTENCES

Set A

1. There is a pond next to our house.
2. The crowd liked the wonderful clown.
3. A powerful storm hit south of town.
4. I found insects eating the flowers.
5. Snakes shed their skin all around the ground.
6. The ant crawls up and down the mound of dirt.

Set B

1. A brown mouse crawls into a hole in the wall.
2. The sound of the band downtown was wonderful.
3. Cats prowl at night and have powerful legs to pounce on other animals.
4. Now the tadpole will shed its skin and get a wide mouth.
5. I give a loud shout when I see insects.
6. Mary saw an owl by the round pond.

Set C

1. The cowboy said that riding in the mountains is wonderful.
2. Kate saw flying insects around the old couch in the garage.
3. It became cloudy by the time we found the pond.
4. A powerful tornado was seen at about noon and scared the crowd of people at the fair.
5. A tadpole's mouth becomes wide, and it will shed its tadpole skin before coming out of the water.
6. How proud Mom seems since the baby now crawls.

© Pearson Education

Two Clowns

The circus came to town last week. It was great   10
fun. There were two clowns who really made us   19
laugh. One was Slouchy, and the other was   27
Grouchy. The crowd howled when they rode   34
around in their little cars chasing each other.   42

Both clowns wore clown suits with cute hats.   50
Slouchy had a tall red hat with a small brim, but   61
Grouchy had a flat green hat with a large brim. They   72
both had big red mouths. Slouchy's mouth was a   81
smile, but Grouchy's mouth was a frown. Their   89
shoes were different too. Slouchy had shoes that   97
made him bounce from place to place. Grouchy's   105
shoes were bigger and turned up at the toes.   114

We watched all the acts for two hours. It was   124
amazing how the clowns could do so many funny   133
things and yet never make a sound. They just ran   143
round and round acting silly. What fun it was!   152

© Pearson Education

READ THE SENTENCES

1. The boy cried tears of joy.
2. Roy ran down the block to join his friend.
3. The giant toy made a lot of noise.
4. It wasn't fair that the loyal cowboy had trouble.
5. Dad didn't chuckle when he spilled oil on the foil.
6. Troy put the coins in a strong box.

Set B

1. Trouble with a giant coil set off a big noise.
2. The metal joint was strong but needed oil.
3. Joy's face was moist with tears when she broke her toy.
4. They planted soybeans in the soil down the block.
5. It isn't fair that the rain will spoil Floyd's picnic.
6. Did you chuckle when the cowboy dropped the coins?

Set C

1. Nothing could destroy the giant wall around the royal palace.
2. Joyce had to chuckle when she burned the steak she was broiling.
3. There was joyful noise during our block party.
4. The coin toss was a fair way for the boys to decide who would go first.
5. Tears ran down the cook's face when his soybeans boiled over onto the stove.
6. Royce had trouble wrapping the oily potatoes in foil.

© Pearson Education

Roy the Cowboy

Roy was a cowboy. He had one problem. He   9
could not eat much of the food that the other   19
cowboys ate. So, he ate soybeans.   25

In the morning, Roy fried soybeans in a little oil.   35
He had boiled soybeans for lunch. He ate mashed   44
soybeans for dinner. For snacks, he ate dry   52
roasted soybeans.   54

One cowboy asked, "Roy, why do you eat so   63
many soybeans?"   65

"Well, I do not eat meat. I enjoy eating   74
soybeans. They are tasty and good for you. And   83
they do not spoil in my saddlebag."   90

But one day Roy did get tired of eating   99
soybeans. He wanted something else. His wife,   106
Joy, packed some mush wrapped in foil.   113

At first Roy liked the mush. So all Roy ate was   124
mush, mush, and more mush until he couldn't eat   133
another bite of it.   137

Now Roy is back to eating soybeans. But every   146
once in a while, he eats a little mush—just for   157
something different.   159

© Pearson Education

READ THE SENTENCES

Set A

1. She clung like glue to her new bike.
2. Our school had a picnic at noon.
3. The angry wind blew a few trees down.
4. The smooth fruit hung from the tree branches.
5. The big blue blooms made the flowers special.
6. I was pressing grapes with a spoon to make juice.

Set B

1. She sat on a stool in the cool shade of branches.
2. He wore his special blue suit to the party.
3. Sue was pressing her fingers along the side of the pool to hold on.
4. Soon we will have a picnic at the zoo.
5. The angry sea tossed the food and the crew all around the ship.
6. The dew clung to the leaves and the fruit.

Set C

1. Some were angry and did not believe the news of the school closing, but they found out it was true.
2. My cat clung to the branches and wasn't in the mood to get down anytime soon.
3. Our fingers held the rail as we looked at the moon and stars from the deck of the cruise ship.
4. His nephew drew a special picture of the town.
5. Stew is not a good food to take on a picnic.
6. Mom knew that pressing the shirt would make it look like new.

© Pearson Education

Sue's Blue Moon

I learned a few facts about the moon in school.   10
When there is a full moon, we can see the whole   21
side of the moon. I think full moons are beautiful! If   32
a moon is a new moon, we cannot see it. Our   43
planet is blocking the sun's light.   49

Do you know what "once in a blue moon"   58
means? It means that something happens only   65
once in a while. Is it true that the moon is really   77
blue? No. When there are two full moons in one   87
month, the second one is called a blue moon. If   97
there is a blue moon, you will not see one again   108
very soon. You will have to wait over two years for   119
it to happen again. Everyone should see the next   128
blue moon. It will be so cool!   135

Once when I was on a cruise ship, I saw a full   147
moon. I drew a picture of it. I think it's a great   159
picture. I call it "Sue's Blue Moon."   166

© Pearson Education

Sentence Reading Chart

Unit 4

	Phonics		Lesson Vocabulary		Reteach ✓	Reassess: Words Correct
	Total Words	Words Correct	Total Words	Words Correct		
Week 1 *The Quilt Story* A B C						
Syllables C + *le*	4					
Lesson Vocabulary			2			
Week 2 *Life Cycle of a Pumpkin* A B C						
Vowels *oo, u*	4					
Lesson Vocabulary			2			
Week 3 *Frogs* A B C						
Diphthongs *ou, ow/ou/*	4					
Lesson Vocabulary			2			
Week 4 *I Like Where I Am* A B C						
Diphthongs *oi, oy*	4					
Lesson Vocabulary			2			
Week 5 *Helen Keller and the Big Storm* A B C						
Vowels *oo, ue, ew, ui*	4					
Lesson Vocabulary			2			
Unit Scores	20		10			

- **RECORD SCORES** Use this chart to record scores for the Day 5 Sentence Reading Assessment. Circle A, B, or C to record which set of sentences was used.
- **RETEACH PHONICS SKILLS** If the child is unable to read all the tested phonics words, then reteach the phonics skills using the Reteach lessons on pp. DI·64–DI·68.

- **PRACTICE LESSON VOCABULARY** If the child is unable to read all the tested high-frequency words, then provide additional practice for the week's words. See pp. 40e, 64e, 94e, 122e, and 148e.
- **REASSESS** Use the same set of sentences or an easier set for reassessment.

© Pearson Education

READ THE SENTENCES

Set A

1. The bus driver slowly left the station.
2. The worker sadly looked at the burning building.
3. Face masks are helpful to firefighters.
4. The roar of thunder woke the campers nightly.
5. The hopeful sailor quickly jumped on the boat.
6. The graceful rider held tightly to the horse.

Set B

1. The deadly tiger's roar made the trainer fearful.
2. The cheerful actors wore funny masks backstage.
3. The ranchers made a brightly burning campfire.
4. The painters quickly finished the beautiful building.
5. The skillful player held on tightly to the football.
6. The ticket seller at the station was friendly.

Set C

1. The train conductor at the railroad station was helpful to us when we traveled through the terminal.
2. The batter held onto the bat tightly and was thankful to get a grand slam hit.
3. The singer quickly stopped the roar of the crowd as she began singing the words of a peaceful song.
4. Doctors and nurses wear masks so they don't spread harmful germs to their patients.
5. The candles were burning, and music was playing softly as the visitors ate dinner.
6. The window washers cleaned the filthy panes of glass on the buildings on a weekly basis.

© Pearson Education

Happy Campers at Bat

The Happy Campers had a skillful baseball   7
team. Their trainer had trained them well. Emma   15
was the pitcher. She had a good arm for throwing.   25
The catcher was Megan. She was great at getting   34
runners out at home plate. The team gladly played   43
every day so they would be the best.   51

Today was the last game of the summer. If the   61
Happy Campers won, they would be champs.   68
Many visitors were there to watch. They cheered   76
loudly.   77

It was the last inning. There were two outs. The   87
pitcher threw a fastball. Megan bravely swung the   95
bat. She missed!   98

Megan sadly walked to the bench. She thought   106
her friends would be upset. But good friends are   115
helpful to each other. The players gathered   122
around her.   124

"It's all right," said Emma sweetly. "We know   132
you did the best you could. We are still hopeful.   142
Maybe next year we'll be the champs." Megan felt   151
better.   152

© Pearson Education

READ THE SENTENCES

Set A

1. Lightning flashes made us feel unhappy and unsafe.
2. Tad was unable to unload the boat in the storm.
3. Jean is unafraid of thunder, but she dislikes its noise.
4. We had to reload and retie the rolling pipes.
5. Sam preheats the stove and pours the uncooked food.
6. When the rain pounds down, Val is unhappy as she rechecks the roof.

Set B

1. You may have to renail or rebuild your roof if the rain pounds through it during a storm.
2. Thunder makes his dog unfriendly and distrustful.
3. Dad prepaid to have the lightning rods replaced.
4. Unpack and unroll the tent in case it pours.
5. It's unsafe to unlock the door during lightning.
6. He disagrees that you must repaint the flashes.

Set C

1. You may have to recover lost files if you do not unplug the computer before lightning strikes.
2. Replay the pregame tape after the thunderstorm.
3. Tom must repaint the barn because the rain pounds on it and discolored the wood.
4. After the rain pours down the air feels refreshing and the dirt seems to disappear.
5. It is unclear if we will regroup after the storm.
6. Gail rewrapped the food and the repacked picnic basket when she saw lightning in the sky.

© Pearson Education

Doghouse Redo

Is your pooch unhappy about a dirty doghouse? 8
Does your dog's house need a redo? It's unkind to 18
make him or her stay in a dirty place. Your dog is 30
unable to fix it, so it's up to you. Follow these 41
steps. 42

First, unload all the bones and toys from the 51
inside of the doghouse. Next, prewash the dog's 59
house with just water from a hose to get the dirt 70
off. Then wash it with soapy water. Watch all that 80
dirt disappear. 82

Is the paint on the outside discolored or 90
chipping? If it is, you will have to repaint the 100
outside. Scrape the wood. After that, recover it 108
with some bright paint. Let it dry. 115
Finally, clean or replace the dog's toys, bowls, 123
and blanket. Refill the dog's bowls with food and 132
water. 133

The dog's home is now clean and refreshed. 141
Your pooch will love you for it! 148

© Pearson Education

READ THE SENTENCES

Set A

1. I knew that the lamb had wagged its tail.
2. Ben knows he has to practice tying the knots.
3. The man knelt by the dripping sign.
4. I chased the cat and hurt my knee and thumb.
5. He grabbed wrapping paper from my knapsack.
6. The knight gave the wren a treat.

Set B

1. Jack grabbed the nasty gnat on his wrist.
2. Kyle will practice making designs for wreaths.
3. A plumber used a wrench to fix the dripping pipes.
4. Ginger wagged her tail when Maria knocked on the wrong door.
5. It is known that the dog grabbed the knob.
6. Mops can wreck a room by chewing signs.

Set C

1. I had to practice knitting scarves before making larger wraps, such as shawls.
2. Meg nicked her knuckle with a knife while cutting a treat.
3. I knelt down and grabbed the dripping towel.
4. In the movie, the gnome with the wrinkled skin chased the elf.
5. The knight's dog wagged its tail as he tried to comb its fur.
6. Fish were chewing on bits of the gnarled wood from the wrecked ship.

© Pearson Education

Needles or Knots

Grace was kneeling on the floor playing with the   9
cat. Her grandmother was knitting.   14

"Grandma, I want a hobby. I do not know how   24
to do anything. How do you get a hobby?"   33

"Well, first you find something you enjoy. Then   41
you learn how to do it well. I learned to knit a long   54
time ago. Now knitting is my hobby," she said.   63

"But you are so good at it. I always do   73
everything wrong when I try." Grace wrapped   80
some yarn around her wrist and thumb and tied it   90
in knots. The cat climbed on Grace's knee and   99
batted at the yarn.   103

Grace thought about the pretty designs that   110
Grandma made. "I could never knit like you do,"   119
said Grace.   121

"It takes practice. You can't learn something   128
just by wishing for it," said Grandma. "If you want   138
to learn, I will teach you."   144

Grace thought about what her grandma said   151
and knew what to do. She picked up some   160
knitting needles and said, "I'm ready to start."   168

© Pearson Education

Set A

1. It is tough to phone home while exploring.
2. I wondered if my graph had enough rows.
3. Jake and his truest friend, Phil, always laugh.
4. Her nephew saw an elephant on his adventure.
5. The greatest dolphin was on the rough sea.
6. Ralph took a photo as I climbed the tree.

Set B

1. Which phrase tells about the tough adventure?
2. We had enough time to phone while exploring.
3. I wondered if he got the trophy for his fine photo.
4. Phil began to cough after he ran to the clubhouse.
5. The gopher quickly climbed up the rough hill.
6. Ella laughed when the dolphin made the greatest jump of the day.

Set C

1. Ben took the greatest photo of an elephant on his adventure in Africa.
2. His nephew heard laughter coming from the clubhouse in the backyard.
3. Philip saw horses drinking from a trough while exploring the countryside.
4. The bar graph showed how the numbers of dolphins have climbed into the thousands.
5. I wondered what happened to the mother of the orphaned baby gopher.
6. It was tough when his truest friend moved away, but they talk on the phone often.

© Pearson Education

A Dolphin, an Elephant, and a Gopher

Our teacher asked us to dress up like an animal   10
and give a report. I chose to be a dolphin. My   21
friend Phil wanted to be an elephant, and Ralph   30
decided to be a gopher.   35

Ralph called me on the phone and asked me   44
what sounds gophers make. I said I did not know   54
and told Ralph to read about gophers.   61

On the big day, our teacher took photos of us in   72
our animal suits. My suit was tough to make, but it   83
looked good enough. Phil's suit was really cool.   91
He used sandpaper to make the elephant skin feel   100
rough.   101

After Ralph read his report, he began to cough.   110
He coughed so much that he had to go for some   121
water.   122

After school, I asked Ralph, "Did you ever find   131
out what sounds gophers make?"   136
"No, I still do not know," he said.   144
"Well, I know one thing. Gophers sure do   152
cough a lot!" We laughed all the way home.   161

© Pearson Education

READ THE SENTENCES

Set A

1. The townspeople cut down tall stalks of corn.
2. The signmaker taught Paul how to make letters.
3. It is important that the straw be here by dawn.
4. We will talk about the law this afternoon.
5. Do not blame him because the mall was closed.
6. Draw a picture of your ideas for the wall.

Set B

1. The plumber took the blame for the flaw in the faucet.
2. We saw a hawk high in a tree in the afternoon.
3. It is important to add only a little salt to the sauce.
4. The signmaker painted a small sign for the lawn.
5. Saul had ideas about how to do the laundry better.
6. The townspeople met at the city hall in August.

Set C

1. Paula's plans caught the attention of the townspeople.
2. The author scrawled her ideas on the chalkboard.
3. It is important to walk fast so we don't miss the rocket launch.
4. The signmaker will draw pictures of steaks and sausages on the meat market's sign.
5. Ann wore her shawl in the chilly autumn afternoon.
6. Blame the icy roads for the auto wreck because the driver was not at fault.

© Pearson Education

Sausages to Go

Every August the town of Smallville had a   8
sausage contest to see who could make the best   17
sausages. The people cooked from dawn to dusk.   25
They used salt and pepper and other spices.   33
Some made fine sauces too. Then people walked   41
from stall to stall and ate sausages all day.   50

One year a sly hawk wanted some meat to   59
gnaw on. He thought, "It will be easy to grab   69
sausages in my claws." So the hawk stole link   78
after link. The people were at a meeting and didn't   88
see him. But a little boy named Claude caught the   98
hawk in the act.   102

When the people came back, they all blamed   110
each other for stealing their sausages. The little   118
boy yelled out, "It's not your fault. I saw the hawk   129
do it!"   131

That taught everyone a lesson. From then on,   139
the town always had a "Hawk Watch." Thanks to   148
Claude no one's sausages were ever stolen again.   156

© Pearson Education

Sentence Reading Chart

Unit 5

	Phonics		Lesson Vocabulary		Reteach ✓	Reassess: Words Correct
	Total Words	Words Correct	Total Words	Words Correct		
Week 1 *Firefighter!* A B C						
Suffixes *-ly, -ful, -er, -or*	4					
Lesson Vocabulary			2			
Week 2 *One Dark Night* A B C						
Prefixes *un-, re-, pre-, dis*	4					
Lesson Vocabulary			2			
Week 3 *Bad Dog, Dodger!* A B C						
Silent Consonants	4					
Lesson Vocabulary			2			
Week 4 *Horace and Morris but mostly Dolores* A B C						
ph, gh/f/	4					
Lesson Vocabulary			2			
Week 5 *The Signmaker's Assistant* A B C						
Vowels *aw, au, augh, al*	4					
Lesson Vocabulary			2			
Unit Scores	20		10			

© Pearson Education

- **RECORD SCORES** Use this chart to record scores for the Day 5 Sentence Reading Assessment. Circle A, B, or C to record which set of sentences was used.
- **RETEACH PHONICS SKILLS** If the child is unable to read all the tested phonics words, then reteach the phonics skills using the Reteach lessons on pp. DI·64–DI·68.

- **PRACTICE LESSON VOCABULARY** If the child is unable to read all the tested high-frequency words, then provide additional practice for the week's words. See pp. 178e, 206e, 232e, 262e, and 290e.
- **REASSESS** Use the same set of sentences or an easier set for reassessment.

READ THE SENTENCES

Set A

1. We'd rather she'd play in right field.
2. They don't know if they've heard cheers.
3. I'd like to catch the ball Bill threw, but I won't.
4. I've seen that you've made it to the plate.
5. They're happy the ball sailed to where we're sitting.
6. They'd like it if we've got runners on all the bases.

Set B

1. I don't know if you're going to play in left field.
2. He'd like the new cheers that you've written.
3. She won't notice if you're running to home plate.
4. We'd be happy if she threw it, but she didn't.
5. Who'd like to clean the bases after they're done?
6. We've sailed once, but they'd like to see it again.

Set C

1. Were the cheers the ones they'd hoped we'd perform?
2. They've wanted to play football on this field since we've been a team.
3. I've never caught a ball he threw, but I know you've done it twice.
4. I don't know if she'd be afraid to run to the plate.
5. You should've seen how the ball sailed over the fence and now it won't be caught.
6. You'd think he'd be proud to make a hit with the bases loaded.

© Pearson Education

Luke and Carlos

Luke and Carlos are best friends. They're the   8
same in many ways but different in other ways.   17

They've always lived on the same street.   24
They're both in the second grade. You'd be   32
surprised to know that they each have an older   41
sister and a younger brother. You've probably   48
seen them ride their bikes together. I've seen them   57
play video games together too.   62

They'd like to think that they're the same all the   72
time, but they're not. Luke belongs to a soccer   81
team. He'd rather play soccer than any other   89
sport. Carlos is on a baseball team. I'd guess that   99
he's the best player on the team. Carlos says he   109
won't ever play soccer. Luke says he won't ever   118
play baseball.   120

The boys admit they'd like to play a sport   129
together. But they don't know if they would both   138
like the same sport.   142

Luke says, "We'd like to try playing basketball   150
on the same team. We're both ready to try it this   161
year. I hope it works out."   167

© Pearson Education

READ THE SENTENCES

Set A

1. We shopped and baked for her birthday.
2. The raised flag of America waves in the breezes.
3. Justin likes making up nicknames for friends.
4. The people hoped for and tried to win freedom.
5. The stars are brighter and the moon is shinier.
6. Your stripes are redder and thinner than mine.

Set B

1. Mark traced stripes on the wall before painting it.
2. Hang the largest stars higher than the tinier ones.
3. When Jen flies the flag it reminds her of freedom.
4. Rachel liked funnier, cuter nicknames for her cat.
5. Al baked a cake with sprinkles for Mom's birthday.
6. People like swimming and diving in America.

Set C

1. America has some of the rockiest mountains and greenest valleys you will ever see.
2. Those who have freedom are luckier and happier than those who don't.
3. My older brothers have the shortest and easiest nicknames to remember.
4. The racing car had a flag and stripes glued on it.
5. The stars were twinkling and shining like diamonds.
6. My birthday was the snowiest, coldest day of the year.

© Pearson Education

The Grand Canyon

The Grand Canyon is located in Arizona. It is   9
277 miles long and one mile deep. A river flows   19
through the bottom of the canyon. Many, many   27
years ago the river cut through the rock and   36
formed the canyon. Today, everyone enjoys   42
rafting on the river.   46

The Grand Canyon contains different kinds of   53
plants and animals. There are willow trees as well   62
as cactus plants. You can find foxes, deer,   70
bobcats, chipmunks, and rabbits. We enjoyed   76
watching chipmunks running and rabbits hopping   82
near the canyon trails. In the summer, it is hot. I   93
think it gets hotter than any other place.   101

People like hiking into the Grand Canyon. The   109
trail is slightly sloping as you go down. I think it's   120
easier to take the mule-pack trip. By riding a mule   130
you will not have any worries about tripping. The   139
rock colors are amazing. I think it's the prettiest   148
place you will ever see. Everyone should see this   157
canyon at least one time.   162

© Pearson Education

READ THE SENTENCES

Set A

1. I took a picture of my aunt at the station.
2. A culture in the nation does basket weaving.
3. One section of the bank features paintings.
4. Use caution when moving your favorite fixture.
5. Jordan collects plastic action creatures.
6. Ella gave me a mixture of lotions for a present.

Set B

1. The portions were a mixture of her favorite foods.
2. My aunt has a section of land that is a pasture.
3. Jill collects stamps from nations where she vacations.
4. The present was a picture of a calm nature scene.
5. In the future, Ned will move the sculpture in a basket.
6. The bank was full of motion on election day.

Set C

1. We had a celebration near the train station before my aunt left on her trip.
2. The picture did not capture the beauty of my favorite waterfall.
3. There is only a fraction of my tuition in the bank.
4. I had a notion that the adventure trip might be my birthday present.
5. Luke's arm has a fracture, and he collects signatures on the cast.
6. The basket held a collection of dollhouse furniture.

© Pearson Education

Tyler's Pictures

Tyler likes to take pictures. His mother lets him   9
use her new camera if he is very careful. The   19
camera lets him look at the pictures right after he   29
takes them. If Tyler does not like a photo, he can   40
remove it.   42

Tyler enjoys taking nature pictures of all   49
creatures, large or small. Sometimes he can   56
capture the moment of an animal in motion. These   65
action pictures are great. Once he got a picture of   75
a bird with its wings out.   81

Of course, he must use caution. He never gets   90
too close to an animal that may sting or bite him.   101
Once he thought he was taking a picture of some   111
ladybugs. When he saw the photo, there was a   120
snake curled up under a plant. That's one reason   129
he must be careful.   133

Taking photos is what Tyler likes to do. He   142
keeps a collection of his pictures in a book. Now   152
and then he looks at them and thinks about his   162
future.   163

© Pearson Education

READ THE SENTENCES

Set A

1. The endless smaller trails were useless.
2. The lifeless railroad station was spotless.
3. The cow's illness filled the cowboy with sadness.
4. The tasteless campfire food was harmless.
5. Sickness made the homeless herd of cattle slow.
6. The fearless horse galloped into the darkness.

Set B

1. The cloudless night at the campfire was noiseless.
2. The cowboy galloped on rainless days and slept under the brightness of the moon.
3. The motionless railroad train was hopeless.
4. The helpless herd was clueless about the flood.
5. The dirtless jogging trails have a springy softness.
6. Colorless rocks matched the paleness of the cattle.

Set C

1. It was hopeless trying to escape the loudness of the railroad train.
2. Some were careless due to the herd's quickness.
3. I felt a soreness in my muscles after running on the trails for a fitness workout.
4. The cowboy felt coldness after the campfire went out and the warmness disappeared.
5. Caring for cattle is a thankless job, but the kindness of people makes it happen.
6. The priceless horse galloped into greatness.

© Pearson Education

Maggie's Wish

Maggie wished she had a dog. Her mom said
she couldn't have one because they're too much
trouble. Maggie knew it was useless to keep
asking.

One rainy night, Maggie heard scratching at the
door. There in the darkness sat a little dog with
sadness in its eyes. Maggie took the helpless dog
into the warmness of the house. She dried off the
dog because it was soaking wet.

"May we keep the dog? I think it's homeless."
Maggie asked.

"You have to try to find its owner first," said her
mom.

The little dog was quiet as it slept in a cozy
corner on a blanket. The next day, Maggie put an
ad in the paper. No one claimed the dog.

Maggie's mom let her keep the dog because
Maggie showed it such kindness. Because the
dog's fur had such softness, Maggie named her
Fluffy. Maggie loved her priceless little dog.

9
17
25
26

34
44
53
63
69

78
80

91
92

103
113
122

130
137
145
152

© Pearson Education

READ THE SENTENCES

Set A

1. Do not misuse silver found in the Midwest.
2. At midpoint in the day, a voice misnamed her.
3. It was a mistake to borrow the midsize car.
4. The drum was mispriced at midweek.
5. I lost the mismatched jingle bells in midsummer.
6. She misspoke due to the midday clattering.

Set B

1. I misplaced my silver necklace in midwinter.
2. The midstate band misplaced their drums.
3. We heard her voice misspell the word during the midweek spelling bee.
4. Do not misbehave and jingle the bells at midnight.
5. I misfiled my Midwest map but will borrow one.
6. The clattering at midweek caused Sue to misdate the letter.

Set C

1. Bess miscounted her money and had to borrow some midway through her trip.
2. Deb misunderstood and took the jingle bells to midship.
3. The voice on the radio misled people in the Midwest.
4. There was a misprint about the price of the drum in the Mideast paper.
5. The clattering caused the police to misdirect traffic at midmorning.
6. It was a mistake to drop the silver ring in midair.

The Spelling Bee

Juan lived in a large midwest city. It was   9
midsummer, and he noticed a sign in the library   18
about a spelling bee in one week. The prize was a   29
new bike. He copied the time and day on a piece   40
of paper. Juan was great at spelling. He hardly   49
ever misspelled a word.   53

Juan studied spelling words every day. One day   61
he stayed up until midnight. By midweek, he had   70
learned to spell many new words.   76

On the day of the spelling bee, he was ready by   87
midmorning. He went to the library, but only the   96
workers were there. He checked the sign. Oh, no!   105
He had misprinted the date. The spelling bee   113
wasn't until the next day.   118

Juan tried to look at the bright side. Because he   128
miswrote the day, he'd have one more day to   137
study. So he learned to spell more words and   146
that helped him win the spelling bee! Sometimes a   155
mistake can be a good thing, he thought.   163

© Pearson Education

Sentence Reading Chart Unit 6

	Phonics		Lesson Vocabulary		Reteach ✓	Reassess: Words Correct
	Total Words	Words Correct	Total Words	Words Correct		
Week 1 *Just Like Josh Gibson* A B C						
Contractions *'re, 've, 'd*	4					
Lesson Vocabulary			2			
Week 2 *Red, White and Blue: The Story of the American Flag* A B C						
Base Words and Endings	4					
Lesson Vocabulary			2			
Week 3 *A Birthday Basket for Tía* A B C						
Syllables *-tion, -ture*	4					
Lesson Vocabulary			2			
Week 4 *Cowboys* A B C						
Suffixes *-ness, -less*	4					
Lesson Vocabulary			2			
Week 5 *Jingle Dancer* A B C						
Prefixes *mis-, mid-*	4					
Lesson Vocabulary			2			
Unit Scores	20		10			

- **RECORD SCORES** Use this chart to record scores for the Day 5 Sentence Reading Assessment. Circle A, B, or C to record which set of sentences was used.
- **RETEACH PHONICS SKILLS** If the child is unable to read all the tested phonics words, then reteach the phonics skills using the Reteach lessons on pp. DI·64–DI·68.

- **PRACTICE LESSON VOCABULARY** If the child is unable to read all the tested high-frequency words, then provide additional practice for the week's words. See pp. 320e, 348e, 374e, 406e, and 432e.
- **REASSESS** Use the same set of sentences or an easier set for reassessment.

© Pearson Education